T0114613

A Call To Reason

WESLY GUITEAU

BALBOA.PRESS
A DIVISION OF HAY HOUSE

Balboa Press books may be ordered through booksellers or by contacting:

Balboa Press
A Division of Hay House
1663 Liberty Drive
Bloomington, IN 47403
www.balboapress.com
844-682-1282

Print information available on the last page.

ISBN: 979-8-7652-3339-9 (sc)
ISBN: 979-8-7652-3338-2 (e)

Balboa Press rev. date: 01/11/2024

Special Thanks

First, I would like to thank all those who have made this journey possible, starting with my parents, my kids, my childhood friends, my teachers, mentors, former colleagues, and the various authors that have taken it upon themselves to share their vision of the world and their place in it, through their timeless literary works.

In the world of literature and the many authors that have helped me to find my own literary voice, are great thinkers and philosophers whose names are well known, such as Hagel, Descartes, Jean Paul Sartre, Aristotle, Socrates and Spinoza.

The list also includes great contemporary hommes de plumes:

Frantz Fanon's book: *Peau Noir Masque Blanc* (translation: black skin and white mask), and his famous psychoanalysis of the residual effect of colonization on colonized peoples.

Antenor Firmin: *de L'egalite Des Races Humaines, Anthropology Positive* (Translation: Equality of the human races, positive anthropology) written in response to Joseph Arthur De Gobineau's book: An essay on the Inequality of the human races, which was used as justification for the so-called superiority of the white race over all others. Specific to Gobineau and Antenor Firmin, I must thank the Haitian Author and Youtube presenter, Doctor, Jean Fils-Aime for his detailed presentation on Antenor Firmin's literary works and many other contemporary authors.

CLR James, *The Black Jacobins*, the most accurate depiction of the Haitian revolution of 1804 in the English language.

Al Gore's, *Assault On Reason*, which helped me to acquire a broader understanding of the American political landscape and a better understanding of the issue of global warming.

Thomas Friedman, *The World is Flat,* which helped to broaden my understanding of the Clinton regime's drive toward globalization and its effect on the world economy.

Jared Diamond, *Guns, Germs and Steel*, a transdisciplinary non-fiction book, which argues that differences between societies and societal development arise primarily from geographical causes.

Malcolm Gladwell, *Outliers,* a great investigative piece on the science of success with the great conclusion that it takes on average 10,000 hours for anyone to become an expert on anything.

Plato: *The Republic*, more precisely, book VII, Allegory, which seems to describe our current reality in excruciating details.

This is just a few of the many great authors who have contributed to my evolution as a human being first and as an author and thinker.

Contents

Prologue

Prior to Socrates, came *Parmenides* who held the view that the multiciplicy of existing things, their changing forms and motion, are but an appearance of a single eternal reality.

On the other side of this argument, we found *Heraclitus*, also a pre-Socrates Philosopher, who argued that the world in its totality is characterized by incessant change and that only change as such remains constant. His philosophy described by this famous quote: No Man ever steps in the same river twice, for it is not the same river and he is not the same man.

There was another group of philosophers, from the 5th century BC called the *Sophists*. They were teachers of the art of rhetoric and moral relativists. Their belief was that no one culture had the absolute truth and that one should only follow the law if such law benefits them. Moreover, they argue that only a fool would follow a law that does not serve their interests. The *Sophists* argue that might makes right and that moral laws are not natural law and therefore matters only to those cultures who believe and practice them.

Socrates and Plato were true synthesizers who merged these conflicting views of *Parmenides and Heraclitus* and the *Sophists* and their skepticism to create the one true original philosophy of their own, which forcefully argues for a dualistic view of reality. That of the physical objects in space and time, which manifest itself through our senses. On the other side, exist a different kind of reality, which is the reality that is of pure concepts, which are matters of thoughts and of pure essence in its form. Plato affirmed this truth of a duality of existence in his science of metaphysics. Metaphysics is that branch of philosophy, which reflects upon the nature of fundamental reality. The kind of reality found in pure thoughts and concepts.

Naturally, Plato's philosophy clashed head on with the *Sophists* view of reality. Plato believed in the superior nature of reason and logic and that morality and justice are true virtues. He believes that access to this kind of reason is only possible to those of superior intelligence. The kind of intelligence of intuitive nature that governs those who seek the truth for its sake and not knowledge for dominating others. Plato affirmed that only those with this kind of knowledge with true reason, logic as its foundation and justice and morality as its principles are fit to govern.

In book VII, the Allegory, Plato describes a scene that when reads in its entirety, can best describe the world in which we currently live and it is this very world that I have tried to reveal in this book. A world tantamount to the *Sophists'* view of the world in Plato's Republic. You can find a summary of the *"Allegory"* in the *Index section* page of the book.

Introduction

When I was a child growing up in the Caribbean, I used to have lots of fun at no cost to my-self and my parents. When I did engage in costly activities they were never more than a few dollars or thereabouts, which included a movie and some snacks.

I move to the United States in the early 1990s and even then, regular unleaded gas cost about $0.99 a gallon. For $1,200 to $1,500 a month one could rent a decent single family house in a middle class neighborhood. A night out during the weekend with your girlfriend could take you less $100.

These same things are now out of reach for most people not because they are working less but because their salaries have barely kept up with the rate of inflation. All the while productivity as a measure of economic output have continually increased with all the gains going to the tiny elite who controls everything.

Moreover, societal norms, behavior, perception and conception of life have dramatically shifted to the futile. Countless individuals are working just to consume with irrational exuberance and what is more pervasive is that the forces of the market seem not only encouraging this type of behavior but also promoting it and sometimes forcing it into our psyche completely unaware. To achieve this, numerous smart and technologically capable individuals from various prestigious universities are busy creating algorithms to study human behavior in order to better control it for their benefits.

We are told that we are lucky to be alive in this era of the greatest civilization humankind has ever known, with limitless potential. We have sent men to the moon and back, we have extrapolated as much knowledge from the cosmos as our machines have allowed us. The Hubble telescope, voyager, new horizon, all men made machines sent into the far and deep space to tell us what is out there. We are capable of building supersonic machines, traveling faster then the speed of sound.

Yet, here we are in the deepest most backward economy the world has ever produced. I don't mean backward in terms of productivity, I mean backward in terms of its lack of logic and reason as demonstrated by the growing income inequality and damages done to our planet. Despite basic economic law of the velocity of money that tells us the health of the economy depends of the ability of the masses to have purchasing power thereby facilitate the exchange of goods for services and to allow them a quality of life with their family. Yet they work as hard as ever and able to buy less and less for their hard earned dollars. Moreover, the ability to consume necessary goods and services like food, household products, clothing etc,, has morphed into irrational exuberance. Countless people are spending their hard earned money on things that they either don't need, or already own enough of or hazardous to their health. Despite the scientists telling us that many of our economic activities, industrialization and the transformation of raw materials into usable good for consumption, have irreparable damages to the planet. Scientists have enumerated the problems for us, from air pollution, food and water contamination, species going extinct, all the way to global warming. Yet, we do nothing about these problems. The same science also points us to possible solutions and still, instead of redirecting our resources to resolving these existential threats to ourselves and the planet, we continue down the same path.

This is not a fluke of the system but that these algorithms that are monitoring all of our behaviors, collecting innumerable raw data on us are responsible for these decisions. From Brazilian butt lift, too all kinds of plastic surgery, to new TVs and a new IPhone each year, the urge to shop and spend is constant. The moment a family manage to earn some equity on their house, credit cards and banks send them a barrage of offers every week to borrow against that equity and spent it. Suddenly, there is a need to remodel your kitchen that is barely a few years old, get new furniture, go splurge on a new vacation package etc... the list of things that you can spend that money on goes longer at each offer. The majority of people are incapable of controlling the impulse to spend. Some of them are of the mindset that preclude them from being able to judge correctly and discern between impulsive behavior and rationale thinking.

How many of us can say categorically that we have an air tight budget that takes care of our needs such as house mortgage, car notes, insurance, taxes, household bills such as food, cable, electricity, phone and ascribe a percentage of our income to savings each month. And do so year in and year out without succumbing to these nice offers from the banks and the credit cards companies.

This is the economic model that this so called greatest civilization has assigned to us all as the best economic and social model for all time and to allow those on top to lead us blindfolded to whatever destination they do chose.

The time is now for a new economic model that takes into account a series of correction into our perception, conception of life, our consciousness, social behavior, moral aptitude and ethical norms.

This is what I will seek to unpack in this book. What is the greatest challenge to mankind in the 21st century, we have the knowledge at least enough of it to make life enjoyable for the majority but we are not using it for that purpose. We are still marred in the old mentality of feudalism, slavery and class where a small group seek to impose its will on all humanity through coercion, or by force has has been the case so often in human history.

I

The social Media Trap

Starting with the basic premise that nothing is free, we engage in innocent social interaction through modern technology unaware of the real objective of these tools and companies that created them.

As a child growing up, social interaction meant calling your friend to get together and plan the day. For most of us, a phone was not even necessary, we simply walk to the next block to pick one and another and slowly the group is formed. A few minutes later a vote is taken that today we will do x or y as activities. Some of these activities usually were physical in nature, soccer, running, swimming or simply enjoying each other's company in long chats about anything and everything. As boys, we may exchange opinion on our newest girls of interest, ask for advise on the best way to impress a girlfriend. As we get older, the conversations got deeper, social issues, politics, economics or pertinent issues of our time.

Today more and more people have relinquished these face to face interactions for remote gathering on face book, Twitter, Instagram and similar platforms. Moreover, because these interactions are now remote, there is a degree of psychological freedom for people to express themselves differently then they would normally have in face to face exchanges. Thus, gradually our norms and behaviors and moral compass change to more vulgarity, gossip, backstabbing, not to mention explicit pictures that are now part of the exchanges.

We do these things in the assumption that these pictures and texts and conversations will remain private and since they are private we then unload our private thoughts on these platforms not knowing that we are being monitored.

When you sign on to these platforms, we willingly give up our identity to these anonymous platforms, name, address, phone numbers, social security and date of birth. The documents required to sign on these platforms alone is a treasure trove for these companies. Gradually, a digital fingerprint is created for each and everyone of us. Overtime, the algorithms that run these platforms extrapolate, analyze and dissect the data they are collecting from us for multiple reasons.

First everything collected can be monetized. Our personal information, which we thought were kept private is now being sold to the highest bidder. They subdivide us into small markets, such as young based on age brackets, professions, class, race, religion, personal taste, income brackets, sexual orientation, political affiliation, level of education etc.

Buyers for this information includes all the major companies that are buying and selling goods and services such as Banks, insurance companies, supermarket, clothing companies, real estate, electronic companies, internet service providers, universities, healthcare companies, pharmaceutical companies, car manufacturers, etc. Each one of these economic actors require a specific set of data on us for their specific product.

Let us dissect our social media digital fingerprint to see what kind of information is typically available to these companies. When I am done, I will show you through careful analysis and observation how each one of these data sets can be monetized and by which industry or economic actors or markets, and how they use our data to make billions.

Banks

If a bank for example wants to know our income bracket, education level, and credit worthiness, they can collect it from their existing pool of customers but that is limiting their access to new potential customers. Therefore new data on new potential customers are required. To achieve this there are two sources of new data to pull from, social media and what is allowed through data sharing arrangements with third party vendors.

Let's look at social media and how they benefit from this data. These financial institutions have powerful data analytics tools capable of dissecting the raw data into specific market segments and assign specific product tailored to each market (keep in mind when I use the word market, I am referring to buyers, of their products, in other words, us). sometimes new products are created based on what type of information the data is providing. Social media is the richest and biggest source of data on potential new customers.

Facebook alone has over 2 billion users globally and growing. The information we use to sign into these platforms is enough for these banks to market their products to us. This is what the industry refer to as generic data with limited potential. The rich data is the behavioral data, the kind that helps data analysts to peek inside our brain to know what we are thinking before we even think it and through more sophisticated platform, they may even manipulate your thoughts at the subconscious level.

The behavioral data is a goldmine to these companies. Behavioral data is what Facebook is good at. You see, Facebook, combine with the smart phone work in tandem. The phone is constantly tabulating your time spent on it, what websites you are visiting, which one you visit more often then others, how many visits is required before you make a purchase. It then keep record of what financial institution you use to make the purchase, which means, credit card, debit card. Do you use gold card, black card and cheaper sources of credits.

Furthermore, the numbers on your credit card or bank account are in themselves a source of hidden codes to the algorithms, just like your social security number and or your license number. Algorithm uses numbers and numbers is the universal language of knowledge but only the machines speak that language.

To must human numbers are just that, a way to compute and derive sums, quantity and in some rare cases to identify things or people but must people don't know that for each one of these categories the machine doing the calculation is speaking in code to each other. A set of digits and carefully calibrated sequence hides specific message that only the machine can decode and or highly trained individuals can know.

Within these numbers are things like, your income bracket, your country of origin, political affiliation, purchasing power, credit worthiness, and many more. Add to this list everything you have ever done on social media.

As someone who has made it a point not to use these platforms. I am not well place to identify what sort of things people do on Facebook or what sort of videos they are posting on you tube. However, as you know, social media is so prolific these days that even if you are not using their platforms, you are constantly bombarded with links, clips, texts from your friends and colleagues and just from there I have tabulated a few things that I've seen, they include but are in no way a complete list of social media content:

- Family photos
- Pictures from vacation accompanied with live video clips of their vacation activities
- New shopping list both before and after the purchase
- The name of their hotel, room number and length of stay
- Picture of their house with the street address
- Picture of their car or cars with the license plate glaring
- A doctor's visit either before or after or sometimes live streaming the reason and the outcome

- Medication they are taking
- What school their kids are attending
- Their kids sports team and social calendar.
- Preparing for an exam, whether work related or for academic purposes
- Mood swings, when they are feeling happy or sad and why
- Exercise and diet not on rare occasion but every time they use the gym or eat something healthy

The list is long, for I have not even begun to list the sort of private activities that I have seen about plastic surgery, in private areas, new tattoos some of which in highly private areas of their bodies, all the way to actual soft porn.

To each and everyone of these posts over a week, a month, a year and multiple years, the data analysts through powerful algorithms can easily and with accuracy, pinpoint the number of times you have visited or posted or purchased something. How many times a day, a week, a month and over the year and with that data they can extrapolate your next move, they can identify your mood happy or sad and when.

For example, you definitely don't know it because you are not keeping track of your post and even if you are keeping track of your post, the reason for keeping track is entirely different for the companies monitoring and mining your data. You are keeping track of how many comments you got on each individual post, likes and dislikes, love, share, etc... for positive reinforcement. They are keeping track of what you are doing routinely for the purpose of being able to accurately identify your personality type, predict with pinpoint accuracy your behavior and your next move and ultimately to be able to shape it to their purpose and objective.

Moreover, no matter how smart you are you can not decode certain hidden correlation between one post or another, and the number of time you may have posted something similar but these powerful algorithms are built to recognize these patterns and trends in the entire set of data.

Let me be more specific. When you pull your smart phone, you scroll and you see dozens and depending on how often and how much time you spend on social media you may have hundreds of new posts coming at you everyday and you may even respond to each one of them and posted as often yourself. To you each post stand alone, sometimes, you might even see a small package from Facebook, arranging your photos for you with specific date and times and they may send you a reminder to say, last year this time, this is where you were and this is what you were doing and who you were doing it with. Well, this is a tiny example of what the algorithm is capable of doing on its own and what they are sharing with you is the mundane stuff, the innocent stuff, which most likely will put a smile on your face.

Take this capability and multiply it a thousand fold and you get an idea how the data analysts can see trends and patterns in things that you don't even know about yourself. Imagine a post about your mood, something to the effect: today, I am happy because..... or today I am sad because ...... well how many times have you posted such comment, when, and what were you doing before such post and what do you do after such post. Based on this information, only you will not know it, but an add or an offer will pop in your inbox automatically as a cure to the state of mind you are in at the time.

By extrapolating and correlating the different data set points, they know when you will be happy and when you will be sad and moreover, they will know what is the best remedy for each state of mind. Each of these remedies is a vulnerable point and a perfect opportunity for service providers to make you do something that you have no idea you were going to do or had no plan to do that day. All of this is happening everyday, hundreds of time to billions of people across the world and none of them have a clue.

They think, it is their idea to go ahead and buy this car, this new dress, new pair of shoes, new phone, new TV, remodel the kitchen, go to the movies, eat at this restaurant or that restaurant, try this new wine, new popular drink, cocktail, do watch this tv series or that tv series. If you don't have the time, because you are busy working long hours to afford all of these activities which you are being prompted to do completely unaware, then buy this new device which can help to record hundreds of hours of your favorite show for you so that when you do have a little of free time. Never mind that you could have used it to pick up a book and read it from start to finish, or spend quality time with your family, instead you are still programmed to be constantly hooked from the moment you wake up to the moment you go to bed.

Insurance companies

Insurance companies seek data to better price their insurance products and to also target specific groups either for better products or for tailored policy terms. For example, did you know that your premium for your car insurance depends on your zip code? If you are an astute individual perhaps you already know this, but do you know why and how? The data they collect on insurance claims, accidents, and the private data you share in your social media platform can tell them if you are a responsible driver or not.

If you live in certain neighborhood they can dissect the data by zip code to see where most of the claims emanate from and what type of claims. All of this data allow them to offer tailored packages by zip code, class, ethnicity. For example, some neighborhoods are more prone to theft than others. Other neighborhoods have higher density of population, narrower streets, high rise apartment complexes, with limited parking space. These neighborhoods are more likely to see small but frequent accidents, such as broken review mirrors, hit and run, while your car is parked on the street, or higher volume of personal properties stolen from your car etc. Meanwhile in higher income neighborhoods, where houses have private parking space for all cars, indoor garages, these types of accidents are highly unlikely to occur and if they do, it is more ad hoc and infrequent.

Based on this data, people who live in certain zip code with a worse driving record then you might get a much better insurance package then you. A better insurance packet includes higher limit, lower premium, lower deductible, and less restrictive terms whereas someone else in a lower income neighborhood with a better driving record will pay more in premium, with higher deductible, lesser limits and much more restrictive terms. Before the monetization of of data through these data analytics tools, insurance companies used to derive their premiums the old fashion but more ethical way, like individual merits.

By that I mean, each insurance policy would be a direct result of the driver's personal record. He who has more accident then the other would pay more and inversely, the driver with less accidents would pay less. Now, data analytics have made it possible for us to be locked in brackets based on stereotypes, and anecdotal data irrelevant to the pricing structure or the risk specific to the driver of that car. Because of this data based product, someone who is an alcoholic or frequent drug user, may have a higher chance of driving under the influence and yet will pay a lot less in premium because he or she happened to live a higher income neighborhood. Meanwhile, someone, who is more socially responsible will pay a lot more insurance just by virtue of his or her zip code.

Pharmaceutical companies

To most people, we have a powerful institution call FDA the food and drugs administration whose job it is to monitor and regulate the food and drugs industry. This institution is the gate keeper for all such products that enters the market. Because of this regulatory body, pharmaceutical companies are forced to follow certain procedures to make sure their drugs are safe before it enters the market for consumption. Indeed some of the policies and procedures include stringent and costly research and development, clinical trials at every stages of development of the drug.

When a drug finally enters the market, it is deem safe for consumption. Indeed must drugs in the market have met this rigorous requirement. However this does not stop the pharmaceutical industry from circumventing these regulatory restrictions. They do so buy investing billions in lobbying congress to help them create loop holes allowing them to increase their profit margins. You might ask what does that got to do with social media, well, be patient I am getting to it. A standard drug that requires a doctor prescription would fall under these rules.

Companies who spend billions to develop a drug will do all that is legally possible to maximize their profit on that drug. To achieve this, a few things are set in place. First they make sure they follow the FDA guidelines to avoid costly fines, these guidelines are the reason why some drugs are very efficient at alleviating certain symptoms in the first place, note that I carefully said alleviating symptoms, because the model for pharmaceutical companies is to do just that, to help people learn how to live with diseases rather then outright cure them. This economic model is predicated on the fact that, a cured patient is a one time customer but a chronically ill patient is a lifetime customer.

This is not to say that there are no drugs capable of curing certain diseases, it is simply to say that economic model exist in the pharmaceutical industry and it is more pervasive then one might think. The business model includes several steps to profitability, once R&D is done, the clinical trial is over, the data analysts come into the picture to help set the price. The price of that drug will be a combination of the R&D cost, the estimated number of people with the disease, the lifetime treatment plan. The latter is where the space for increasing profit exist. At the clinical trial level, data is collected continuously to monitor the dosage and to determine the right dosage to give.

Well, some companies have manipulated the dosage data to make it possible for a longer lifetime treatment plan, thus securing a source of profitable products in the market for the longest time possible until, a competitor comes up with something better.

Where a drug is proving to be less effective, by that I mean mildly alleviating the symptoms while creating a long list of side effects and health complication to the patients, such drug is not removed from the market but instead a decision is made to buy costly insurance to protect the company from the expected law suits. This is called a cost and benefits analysis. Usually the cost of that insurance is also included in the price of that drug. Expected losses from side effects, complications and potential recall all are part of that cost and benefits analysis.

The pharmaceutical companies then collects data routinely on the users of that drug to help them monitor the side effects on race, class, ethnicity and gender basis and sometimes this is factor in at the clinical trial level where the drug is tested prior to hitting the market. This is why a lot of the clinical trials for these companies are conducted outside the country, usually in third world countries where the liability laws are either non existent or easier to circumvent.

Moreover, the science of pharmacy does have a race base component to it. Certain race of people are more prone or more susceptible to specific illnesses, such as sickle cell anemia is know to be more common in blacks.

Another example is an individual's race or ethnic background could be a determining factor when it comes to risk of atrial fibrillation, the most frequently diagnosed type of irregular heart rhythm, according to a new study at UC San Francisco.

Researchers discovered that self-described non-Hispanic whites are more likely to develop atrial fibrillation than people from other race or ethnic groups.

"We found that consistently, every other race had a statistically significant lower risk of atrial fibrillation compared to whites," said senior author Gregory Marcus, MD, an associate professor of medicine who specializes in electrophysiology in the UCSF Division of Cardiology. "So this suggests that white race is itself a risk factor for atrial fibrillation."

In this case the data collected is from a more reputable Chanel and for more scientific purpose then actual further marketization purposes. Data is collected to monitor the patient responses to the drug and such data is also dissected by race, ethnicity to see how each group respond to a specific drug. It is precisely this data that allowed the University of San Francisco to publish this study.

For more information on this subject, please visit www.gwenOlsen.com. She is a 15 year veteran of the Pharmaceutical industry with extensive knowledge on the issue.

Supermarket

Here, we are not referring to your mom and pop corner store, we are talking about the big conglomerates with hundreds of stores across the country some of which requires special membership to purchase their merchandises.

These supermarkets also use data analytics to sell to their customers although at a much lower rate than the other economic entities. Your supermarket access to data is less pervasive in nature, less harmful to your health depending on your diet but it is nonetheless another chain in the overall system of control and behavior control. You might say there is no harm in receiving an add to go grocery shopping or there is nothing wrong with receiving coupons and discounts for specific products. Indeed, you are right.

Like the small package from Facebook reminding you of where you were on a specific date with whom and what you were doing, putting a smile on you face, a clip of coupon or discount to go grocery shopping may do the same. However, do you know that your eating habit is also monitored so that you may buy certain stuff more than others. Do you know that data can also be shared with other parties for their own purpose.

Usually, in these supermarkets, all you need is an application on your phone like most online shopping experience these days. With this application you can browse and shop at your leisure.

The physical infrastructure of the supermarket at first offers the shopper nothing different then a traditional supermarket, perhaps The esthetic might make you feel that you are in a different store and the shopping experience tells you that this a futuristic shopping experience.

However, hidden behind all of this is the infrastructure that makes it all possible. This infrastructure is uniquely design for one purpose to monitor your behavior, eating habits, likes and dislikes, financial institutions used to effectuate your purchase, when you buy, how much you buy, do you buy for one person, two, three or more, does your family include teenagers, toddlers, babies, pets or all adults. How much do you buy and how long does it last? To gather all of this information a network is needed and that network is everywhere in the building. There are the cameras you can see and those that are not visible to the naked eye.

The ceiling has all kinds of censors and cameras monitoring your every single move and tabulating it all to comprise a story, a narrative on you and your family.

Moreover, the nefarious aspect of this shopping experience is the fact that the data collected on each shopper does not serve only the supermarket purposes, let's say to make your shopping experience more enjoyable or to help you shop more diligently and with less inconveniences.

This is likely the front story when introducing the idea and their effort to convince people to join them but the real story, the real purpose is the collective data dump and the sharing of that data with other institutions that you use throughout your life. Through your online supermarket shopping experience, the data collected provides a clear view of your family make up. That data will then tell other economic actors what potential customers exist or live at that address. They will know if you live alone, have teenagers, other adults, infants, doodlers, pets, and each one of them will be targeted for new products from multiple vendors. This is done through a massive data collection across multiple disciplines. Thus, you now have an idea what is happening between your social media fingerprint, your supermarket shopping experience, your banking, insurance, healthcare, restaurant, vacation with friends and family alike. In the end when this global project is done, nothing will be left outside of the parameters of this system of control.

The Artificial Intelligence behind the Data

To give you a more technical understanding of what I am saying, let me give you a little tour behind the scene of the so called Artificial Intelligence in use to accomplish this mission. It is called quantum computing or quantum mechanics.

If you don't know what quantum mechanics is, don't worry, you are not alone. I too had limited understanding of it until recently when I force myself to research and study it.

The quantum mechanics is just a computing system but unlike a regular computer that uses values of 1 and 0 to calculate, quantum mechanics also uses values in between 1 and 0, thus making more efficient and more accurate in its calculation. It also allows it to speed up the process by a huge factor. According to an article published on livescience.com, by Mark Smith on March 18, 2022, quantum computer is 158 million times faster then the most sophisticated computer. It can do in four minutes what it would take a traditional computer 10,000 years to do. With this level of speed the entire planet of 7.5 billion people are just a tiny spec of what this can do.

A better way of explaining this is the science of data analytics, which is the technical term given to the functionality of quantum computing. Data analytics is now at the center of our economic and social activities. Data is collected by everyone and one everyone and the analysis are being done to extrapolate whatever a given party desires. For a Data analyst, data is the tool he or she uses to accomplish his or her work. Data is to quantum computing what flour is to bread. The more data the better.

Thus taken individually, these companies who are collecting data on us seem innocuous, and the story they tell us everyday to convince us to acquiesce to their global project of mind control, behavior control is a good one. Like propagandas, they bombard us daily with feel good stories and they even invent new buzz words to drive home the message. We are told that this is to enhance your shopping experience, to make this activity or that activity a more pleasant experience for the customer or to drive efficiency thus allowing us more free time with our family. To further convince us and hide their true agenda, they replace words like "advertisement with the word "engagement". Thus we don't believe that we are being sold to, but rather engage in social interaction with our peers.

On the surface and with a cursory analysis you can't find fault in what they are saying because when you look at it from that perspective it all adds up. A typical grocery shopping trip could take you hours to complete, a typical trip to the mall could take hours to complete, etc... when you add it all up, it makes sense. Rather then spending all of these hours of your days waiting on line at this store or that store, you now have the ability to accomplish all of this at the click of your mouse at home and even better right there on your phone, while watching your favorite show. It all make sense.

However, when you look beyond the veil, and take a pick at the full story. A completely different picture emerges and it is not one that would drive comfort, convenience and confidence in the system that is taken shape around us, completely unaware.

The picture that emerges behind the veil is one of a global project for a uniformity of thoughts, wants desires, ideas and feelings. Thus rendering us all more robot then human, completely at their mercy to manipulate us. The technical terms for that is "controllable quantum state" which means to the AI (artificial intelligence) we are just "qbits" and the more people are brought to this quantum state of qbits the more accurate and the more efficient the system can run itself on automatic pilot and unencumbered. A state of control where there is no outside forces to challenge it, no new ideas to emerge from what we free thinkers call the dialectical process of thinking.

The idea of having a debate centered around a few controversial and conflicting ideas, What Hegel called dialectical thinking which consist of the process of arriving to the truth, the ideal, through the clashes of ideas. Commonly referred to as the famous triad: thesis, antithesis and synthesis. The process of dialectical thinking allows room for competing ideas to debate each other in a free unencumbered format and may the best idea wins. The process of arriving at the best idea is not through coercion, force, lies, manipulation and control but rather through well thought out ideas, reason and logic, all of which we are at risk of losing forever, if we allow this global project to take shape unchallenged.

15 Seconds of fame

It was in spring 2003 and I was at the time a junior broker at one of the prestigious brokerage firm in the world. We were invited to a healthcare conference to take part in the annual Ashrm (American society of healthcare risk managers) which host a long list of top healthcare executives at different levels of the industry but mostly hospital risk managers, CEOs and CFOs pharmaceutical companies and top level physicians involved in both risk management and care dispensation.

This annual event is a jewel for this industry with a clear inside view of the inner workings of the health care industry at all its levels. It makes possible for these executives to compare and contrast the strategies implemented at their respective institutions and where necessary to be able to effectuate change in a continuous effort to reduce medical errors, an insurmountable challenge given the complexity of the science of the human body but a noble goal nonetheless.

It was during one of these conferences that I went to New Orleans for the first time. I did not know what to expect but I knew for example the shared history between Haiti and Louisiana as the state where most of the free people of colors, some of the slave masters and other freed slaves migrated to in the aftermath of the Haitian revolution that lead to the independent state of Haiti in 1804.

This shared history also tells me that it was because of the Haitian revolution that the US was able to almost double its size through the Louisiana purchase from France. Napoleon had no choice but to sell Louisiana to the US as he was deprived of its most valuable and profitable colony St Domingue, which wealth he used to fund its military campaign across Europe.

Unfortunately rather then recognizing this debt of gratitude toward Haiti, America has allowed Haiti, which is just about a couple of hours flight to Florida to exist in a continuing state of chaos and poverty, next to the richest country on earth. According to a recent New York Times article, instead of friendly neighborhood trade and economic interaction, Washington partnered with France in creating the very poverty that we see in Haiti today. For more information on this subject, I refer you to the recent NY Times article by Emmett Lindner published on May 22,2022, with the title "Investigating Haiti's double debt."

There I was in the beautiful French quarter of New Orleans. We stayed in a push and luxurious hotel in the financial district and to my surprise the next day I was approached by a film crew to participate in their commercial or add. I thought for a brief moment I was going to be in a film but I was advised that it was a commercial and I was simply to be in the background as a visitor to the area and hotel guest, which I was. For this purpose and because they could not cordon off the hotel lobby they had to pretend we were in the footage and for that brief several seconds of appearance on camera, they had to make us sign a disclosure agreement and a hold harmless agreement that we agreed voluntarily to let our image be used for this commercial.

The next day we all made it to the French quarter where all the fun is. There we saw amazing performers, street performers and great marching band and the sound of jazz was everywhere. I also ate great see food like oyster, clams prepared several different ways, raw on the

Half shell, stuffed with mushrooms, baked with spices etc... the next day I attended a few sessions of the conference and that evening I took the flight back home.

A few weeks later I had a copy of the commercial. My appearance was brief just how they promised and I was just walking across the lobby holding my brief case.

The reason I shared this story is to show you how much the world has changed since 1995. Today, cameras are everywhere in the streets, the mall, the restaurants, the stores, the schools and most prolifically in hand held devices where we are been monitored constantly by everyone and our images unbeknownst to us are everywhere on Facebook, Instagram, twitter and YouTube, whether it is at a friends party or at your own house.

People are always filming each other for their own use and policing and controlling your image, as was the case for the commercial, becomes an impossible task. The only thing left now is not to appear voluntarily, meaning offering comments or other signs of tacit approval. If someone films you while you are casually dancing but had no clue of the act or while walking, eating, shopping unaware of the camera it's one thing, otherwise you acknowledge and agree to be on camera. The viewer can discern that for themselves.

We have to recognize that these algorithms are everywhere. They decide who gets paired up with what jobs on job sites like LinkedIn, indeed and others. They decide who gets the next mortgage and at what rate. They decide who gets admitted to what college, what kind of information you receive on your phone etc. the world as of now is run by machines and the machines are there to exacerbate all the implicit biases that already existed in the society. In other words you can't fix the algorithms without fixing society first.

In the world of big data there is an old saying "garbage in garbage out" this is precisely what we have done with these sophisticated tools be it quantum computing, data analytics and their respective scientists. We have handed over a badly screwed up system over to these machines not to make better decision for us but to accentuate and perpetuate all the inequities, implicit biases, be it race, gender, class, ethnicity and religion. Each and everyone of these sectors are screwed up on a standalone basis but put together what we have now is a giant mess the likes of which the world has never seen before.

One can note the algorithm at work every time an add shows up on your screen for something you did not ask for but was perhaps thinking of or had looked at a few hours ago on a different site. This same algorithm is trained to recognize your pattern at different sites including your likes and dislikes. The objective is to go beyond advertisements. Regular form of advertisement is a one way street. A billboard, a tv add has no way of controlling your response to it. No way to coerce you into buying that product other then your personal taste.

Algorithm is constantly busy feeding you similar adds, videos to keep you "engage" all the while running models in the background to see your mood, your taste, social status, ability to buy something much more expense. And this is just while you watching the add for a few seconds.

For the well trained individual he or she knows not to click on adds unless it was your original intention otherwise the phone is capable of directing how you use it and for what purpose.

Skills lost to your phone

Memory, particularly, people's phone numbers, addresses, direction to and from a place. Before the phone we had no choice but to rely on our memory to remember at least a dozen phone numbers and addresses of our closest friends and family members. When was the last time you pick up the phone and dial someone from a number committed to memory rather then using your phone book or worse by telling Siri to connect you to this or that person. When was the last time you drove more then a few miles outside of your town without GPS(google maps, waze and others) to get you there and in doing so we have become less familiar with the road, the trade marks of directions like landmark, special buildings, stores, distance driven from A to B.

Believe it or not this was or used to be a skill that people had to work hard to develop. It's all gone and as a result we may go to the same places dozens of time and still have no clue what is between point A and point B, we've lost all sense of connection to the land, the places, the fun drives to see new things that are outside of our daily routine. A new building in construction, a different architecture, a park, a bridge, and other things of interest. All these things used to be what makes long distance driving fun and enjoyable.

I used to drive for hours to go see my extended family in Boston and in Montreal, Canada. These were very long trips, but I can not tell you how much I have enjoyed them. I used to look forward to these trips, as a way to reconnect with nature, to see the landscape, to listen to my jazz collection. Depending on the season, you can see the trees and flowers blooming, with a carnival of colors in display for hundreds of miles, or the grip of winter on what was just a few months prior full of life. Now a days with-self driven cars passengers will be fully connected to their phones while driving across states, completely unaware of this beautiful experiences available to all for free. Precisely where and how they want you to behave, to become thoughtless, mindless creatures destine for consumption only.

Social media is also eating away at our ability to speak properly, to use and develop proper communication skills, including a rich vocabulary and the ability to process non verbal cues from the listener(s). We now use less time talking to each other face to face or on the phone and we use fewer and fewer words when we do speak. Our vocabulary is diminishing and we are using the same speech pattern over and over again

We also lose our focus because we no longer trust our instincts to dictate our course of action instead we are prompted by our phone, a

Tweet, a post, a pop up add to act. Focus is high currency skills because he or she who is able to maintain and increase on that skill set will be on high demand in an economy that is more and more depending on high skills jobs. Think of the things you can do with the ability to focus your attention on one thing from start to finish like reading a 350 pages book, or a project of some kind or to write a report, or write a book for that matter.

None of this is to suggest that you should stop your online activities or stop using GPS altogether. It is rather a call, a reminder how to circumvent true automated nature of the system so that you can operate independently of it and not subject to automated actions desires and wants, which is the real goal of the system for automated is easy to maintain and it is perpetual and uncontested.

By balancing out your use of social media between your real wants and needs, you will be able to gain access to other sources of more pertinent information according to your objective and thereby overcome the manipulation for which the algorithms are designed to do. Thus allowing room for your continuing to evolve as an individual, as the human being that you are.

Everyone is afraid of the future and a lot has been said about a future where machines will rule over man. Hollywood is busy reinforcing that fear in us with movies like AI or artificial intelligence, Robocop, cyborg, terminator, I robot etc... What we do not realize even though it is right here in front of our eyes and exposed for all to see is that we are the AI with a small "i".

We live in a digital world where our human instincts are becoming less and less relevant.

We can no longer do simple calculations because we have created a machine to do it for us; called the calculator. We no longer need to learn a foreign language because we have Siri or some other form of computer who can speak for us. Siri how do I say, "The world is crazy in French "le monde est fou". We no longer need to type in the computer forcing us to learn how spell because the computer is now operating by voice command.

Gradually, we are relinquishing our intelligence, our ability to reason, to compute, the very attributes that have made us unique in the cosmos.

Vicious Cycle

Summertime is the most precious of time, especially in America. From Memorial Day weekend that starts the summer with all kinds of fun activities, to its Climax at July 4th weekend, the biggest celebration yet of the summer, all the way to Labor Day weekend to close the summer.

Summertime offers people who perhaps have been locked indoor throughout the summer months, people are busy getting up at dawn to go to work, and come home in the dark, with very little time left in between for personal, social interaction with family and friends.

Suddenly, the days are longer, brighter, sunnier. In the summertime, you can come home from a hard day's work and still have a few hours to sit outside in your backyard for a quick barbecue with family and friends, watch your kids kick the soccer ball on the green grass, or shooting the basketball in the hoops by the side of the driveway. Green grass and beautiful trees everywhere, that a few months earlier were brown or completely dead, watch a multitude of birds of different species galvanizing about, flying from threes to threes, all the while serenading us with their beautiful melodies.

Summertime also gives to those of curious minds and armed with the right intuition a chance to observe the different realities coexisting and evolving around us. One of these set of realities is the observation I made of people that I know, some very well, some not so well, how they are caught in a loop of repetitive behaviors, including vocabularies, conversations, habits and emotions. To the curious mind imbued with the right intuition, it becomes obvious that some have stopped to evolve, some have yet to start while others are busy unlocking the secrets of life and finding answers to the most vexing questions of our existence, as to who are we? Why are we here, where does life come from, who is the architect behind this grandiose experiment, where does our ideas come from? etc..

To illustrate my point, let me share with you a recent observation I made. It is as innocent at observing two birds trying to communicate without gestures. Some bird species used their songs to communicate, and they understand each other exceptionally well, other species use the different colors on their feathers to put on a show to the party of interest. Today, at a human level, many are those who have lost the ability to communicate properly and lack the slightest intellectual curiosity to seek new information, meet new people, engage in different conversation, venture in unfamiliar territories for the purpose of advancing their human experience.

There are people who are caught in the same loop everyday, every week, every month and every year. Watching and observing them is like putting one of my favorite jazz CD on a constant loop to play each song on the list one after the other and when it is done to start over again. After listening to this CD a few times you can easily identify the pattern, you simply know that after this song what comes next. The same is true for those living in these kinds of social bubbles on social media, right wing media, left wing media. The same conversations are repeated over and over again, sprinkled with the appearance of diversity of thought based on a new member of the group, a new event of the day, like a school shooting leading to gun control debate, but in reality, no new information is released, nothing new is revealed. It is the same old debates over and over again, generating passion, animosity, hatred, and in some cases even violence.

Social media is a sort of amplifier of these bubbles making it possible to create the semblance of meeting new people, but really it's an echo chamber where the same ideas are recycled in an infinite loop.

Lean on the past to
build the future

In 1998, I attended a course on public speaking. Part of the curriculum required each student to perform 4 speeches two of which required significant research and visualization. I decided for one of my speech to research the Egyptian civilization. I chose that topic for two reasons; I had heard a lot about the Egyptian civilization but never really studied it. As a black man, I wanted to understand its relevance to my ancestry. Second, I also wanted to learn something new, while also improving my public speaking skills.

That was the best choice for me because it opened my mind to so much and set me on a course to a broader understanding of the world and my place in it.

No one ever told me or told us that the Egyptian civilization was an African civilization by virtue of its geography but also the people. I had to step outside of my college's curriculum to educate myself about it. During my research, I was able to uncover relevant truth about that civilization. The evidence was overwhelming, from paintings of statues, black people with broad noses and kinky hair depicted in the highest echelon of power and prestige, including the many Pharos themselves.

We are fed so many lies for so long and you look around all you see is evidence supporting that lie, you are not a fool for believing that lie, for all the conditions are set for that lie to become your reality.

Along the way, the majority of us voluntarily agree to surrender our voice and all our potential to others, simply because they told us it was the right thing to do. Perhaps, we were born into a society, a culture, a reality that made it normal to devalue ourselves. No one thought us that part of our journey here was to help identify who we are, our purpose, and use it to better yourself and doing so improve the life of others.

The Egyptian civilization and all its potential was lost because they too failed that basic test. Those who had access to the knowledge that led to one of the truly great civilizations on earth, kept that knowledge to themselves in a very small circle of powerful elite, priest, engineers, philosophers and astrologist, medical scientists. They never bothered to create a system to prepare the next generation to transfer that wealth of information.

By the time the Assyrians invaded the Egyptian empire, the Ottoman and the Nubians, it had no way of regenerate itself. Little by little, its identity stolen until there was nothing left. Today, if you want to revisit that era of past glory, you cannot go to Cairo, Egypt. You have to go London and Paris because this is where they keep all the true artifacts capable of retracing the identity and the culture of the époque

Today, we have all the necessary tools to prevent a repeat of such tragedy. With the power of the internet, knowledge can no longer be kept secret from the masses for long. Unfortunately, the powerful elite is always a step ahead. Early on, they recognized this reality and saw the potential risk to their current hegemony. They have devised a successful two Prongs strategy: first to divert our attention away from the important stuff.

We know how well that has worked. An entire generation of people is growing with more power available to them than at any time in the history of man but they are completely oblivious to it because they are too busy playing fortnight, checking Instagram, tweeting, Facebook and whatever this generation is fascinated by these days. College educated kids who should use their college degree as a stepping stone to greater knowledge instead are quickly settled into a routine of 9 to 5 and to busy grinding away in search of a successful career.

When The French Philosopher Renee Descartes coined the Latin phrase: *"cogito ergo sum"* Meaning, "I think therefore I am" he also meant that in order for you to claim your true humanity, you must be able to think for yourself. It is that which separates us from the other species on the planet.

When that ability is gradually reduced to soundbites, incoherent thoughts it is the very essence of our humanity that is imperiled. This is where we are now.

Our insatiable appetite for consuming everything that our senses crave and the economic model that depends on those cravings as a way to generate growth, like scavengers without a conscious is a recipe for disaster.

Everything that we have achieved to this point, we have achieved through the careful deliberation and methodical use of reason and logic. Simply put reason and logic are the sole guarantors of human existence. Reason and logic may well be our only savior yet again to pull us back from precipice.

Everyday, well-meaning people are led to believe that this, the most beautiful most precious thing in the entire universe called intelligent life, which is what we are, intelligent life made of 3 entities: body, soul and spirit. Our elite knows it and that is why after searching the cosmos for signs of intelligent life, they returned with proof that so far, we are it.

You are led to believe that it does not matter much. That you should relinquish your right to self-determination, to freedom of thoughts. I simply want to highlight the gravity of the situation we are in. We need a collective consciousness that forces our elite and various leaders to put up or shut up and let people determine the course of their lives. Until the Architect of the grand experiment himself shows up with a better ideas, we ought to continue to seek to experiment life in this state of awareness.

We must look at ourselves in the mirror each time presented with a challenge or insurmountable problem, and know that which has allowed us to create this world, is the God in us. The God or intelligence who has created us, imbued with such attributes as logic, reason, common sense, ethic, morality, empathy, sympathy. These attributes are at the foundation of who we truly are, as human.

The Green Revolution

Jimmy Carter's 1977 speech on the energy crisis and the policies that followed pave the way for the energy revolution right to present day.

A few years prior, oil prices spiked and from 1973 to 1975, prices were up 5 fold. While most of the major countries in Europe instituted measures to reduce their consumption, America continued to increase its consumption and by 1977, the country was importing 9,000,000 barrels of oil a day, about half of its daily consumption mostly from OPEC (organization of petroleum exporting countries). Furthermore, the five fold increase in price threw a hole in the budget. To put it in perspective, the country spend $25 billions in oil imports, which represented more then its entire export from its farmers. (sources: data extracted from the President speech at The Carter center)

To address this major economic upheaval, Jimmy Carter proposed sweeping changes to the country. First the creation of the energy department with its own energy secretary, a new bill to Congress which accomplished a few milestones, in terms of new law mandating cars be more fuel efficient, increase in domestic oil production, new tax incentives for oil producing companies to increase output and by getting access to new oil fields. More importantly, the stage was set then for the energy revolution we are now seeing in solar, wind, and biofuel.

Today Elon musk is leading the field of renewable energy with his Tesla model, the luxury brand electric vehicle, solar city to power individual homes and businesses alike.

Elon musk example is the continuation of his mentor's legacy, Nicholas Tesla, whose vision of the world includes a body of work that span all aspects of our lives. This American engineer and physicist made dozens of breakthroughs in the production, transmission and application of electric power. He invented the first alternating current (AC) motor and developed AC generation and transmission technology

Most of his innovation and creations don't bare his name. These include, wireless technologies, which is now in everything such as the remote control, radio antennas, wireless telephone, the Global Positioning system, remote control airplane such as the famous predator drones of the military, and the various commercially available drones and many others.

Tesla's dream was to use this technology to provide wireless electricity to the world free of charge. He thought highly of the need of energy as the foundation of the economy and access to boundless electricity would make it much more likely that Individual nations would benefit from such revolution in energy sources and thus tending the world of competing economies a level playing field. The latter statement is from me. It is the inference of such revolutionary ideas would have had in the world. The impact in people's lives across the third world would have been profound indeed. Unfortunately, the powerful elite, small in numbers but powerful in knowledge and resources killed the project before it could take off, simply because they could not profit from it. JP Morgan who was Nicholas Tesla's main financier pulled the plug on him and today, all there is left of Tesla's original work is this Antenna in Long Island New York and even that was recently demolished as to completely erase the idea from our memory. Wardenclyffe Tower (1901–1917), also known as the Tesla Tower, was an early experimental wireless transmission station designed and built by Nikola Tesla on Long Island in 1901–1902, located in the village of Shoreham, New York.

Though Elon Must did not follow the same principle of free access to his products, because, in today's world everything is super expensive and more over, no banks would finance such idea. Musk Space X company came close to running out of money when his first several prototypes falcon X could not successfully take off and land. Several of them exploded on impact and each explosion is millions of dollars in flame. Nonetheless, Tesla's objective need not be abandoned, where free is not realistic or possible cheaper price for these products should be the objective, the raison d'être of both solar city and Tesla.

Space X could still be an expensive enterprise whose objective and vision remains inaccessible to most people, but Tesla and solar city are two business models and innovative ideas which are founded in the noble cause of Nicholas Tesla to give the masses access to energy, the building block of a successful economy thus inexorably will help to extricate and alleviate the plight of the masses much faster then any government could, especially when we know that most government tend to be corrupt and such objective would never be attained if we wait on them to deliver.

In this perspective, both solar city and Tesla would fall short of their objectives of lower carbon emissions if they do not make these products and related services available to all, especially to the third world nations, where the need is the greatest and lack of access energy leads to deforestation, water contamination, land erosion, air pollution through the use of massive amount of diesel fuel.

While space X continue to deliver supply to the space station at a cost significantly less then NASSA, and is now planning ahead with grandiose ideas of putting a colony on Mars, the surplus from space X, especially any potential wealth found On mars or elsewhere in The form of minerals, and other elements of value and even potential new sources of energy supply should be devoted to fund further research and development of both Solar City and Tesla for the simple and most profound objective of realizing his mentor's dream of providing universal access to cheaper renewable energy to the world

Imagine the potential wealth and possibilities of long term sustainable development this could create here on earth not just For a minority but for the peaceful development of all nations.

Cheaper electric cars capable of going fast and far on a single charge with millions of solar charging stations across a vast network across the globe.

Moreover with further research and development at solar city, we could render the cost of solar panel much cheaper and finally cross the threshold of cheaper kilowatt per unit of currency spend in comparison with the status quo and further reduction in cost means affordability by billions across the globe who are now deprived of such basic needs.

The powerful combination of solar city and Tesla and other similar companies could usher in a new era of global prosperity the world has never seen and reduce the existing fault lines between nations competing for finite resources and ready to go to war to secure their supply lines and Willing to destroy innocent countries, especially in the third world, by installing puppet governments to service their malign interest and to destroy their local economy for the benefits of their patron states, such is the main reason the third world can't seem to catch a break. This is done in pursuit of their objective of limitless growth in a world with finite resources.

In the field of transportation alone, the idea of fleets of electric cars, buses and trains that can transport millions across far distances at a fraction of today's cost would be a huge win for underdeveloped and developing countries. Most of these services still remain out of reach to billions across the world. A bus fair, a taxi ride let alone a train ride are still luxuries to billions of our brothers and sisters across the world. More over most of these countries do not have oil and thus continue to export this commodity to power their badly run economy. In Haiti for example, the government subsidizes the electrical company to the tune of $200M a year. To put it in perspective this sum is greater then the national budget for education or healthcare, two critical pillars of any advanced economy and even more so in the developing world because of the lack of access to education by a great percentage of their population. In the case of Haiti, a great deal of progress was made on both cases in education and healthcare simply because of a deal the Haitian Leader, President Rene Préval was able to struck with the then President of Venezuela, Hugo Chavez.

The deal allowed Haiti to buy all its oil from Venezuela at a discount. The initial payment of 25% down and the balance finance at a very low interest rate of 1% for 25 years. This deal allowed the Haitian government to have access to badly needed cash flow to build hundreds of new schools across the country especially in the remote towns and villages where access to education, even at the primary level was a luxury inaccessible to most. To put it in perspective, I recently watch an interview of former Haitian First Lady, Martine Moise, who has my sympathy due to the recent horrific attack on her person in the assassination of her husband, President Jovenel Moise.

She said in that interview that Haiti needs 15,000 new classrooms in order to provide universal access to education and this is just the infrastructure needed. It does not include the cost to run such enterprise which will likely means thousands of new teachers, substitute teachers and other employees and adding millions more to the national budget, which itself is already heavily depending on foreign aid.

A reality impose to the country by the same global elite running this world, for Haiti possess a rich history, thousands of kilometers of empty beach ready for investment and moreover, oil, gold, bauxite, aluminum all part of the Haitian patrimony, but we are unable to exploit these things for our own benefits and by now you should know why and whom is behind all of this sad state of affaires in Haiti, which is a microcosm of the imposed reality of the third world.

President Preval also used some of the funds to buy a fleet of new public buses powered by Venezuela's fuel to help reduce the cost of public transportation and improved access and quality at the same time.

Moreover, the deal allowed the government to reduce the budget deficit and allow less dependence on foreign aid.

Unfortunately, like everything good that happens to Haiti, the elite forces of this world who are hell bent on maintaining the status quo, have found a way to debilitate Venezuela's economy so badly that it can no longer afford to maintain this deal with Haiti and other countries in the region. To that affect Haiti suffered a triple blow, first the earthquake destroyed must of the gains made during Preval's administration, then came a novice of the name Michel Martelly to power forced on the country in a forged election by the international community.

His mission it seems was to boycott the reconstruction effort and allow the same international community free range to siphon the outpouring of aid to the country. Billions for reconstruction disappeared and the Haitian people who had zero access to the money is blamed for its mismanagement. In this case, institutions like the Red Cross are mentioned throughout as actors of that fiasco. But even then, the deal with Venezuela allowed for close to $4B dollars in reserve from the oil deals to help rebuild some aspect of the economy and infrastructure and that money was siphon as well by the imposed leader we got from the international community. Both Martelly and his successor, Moise were inept at best or corrupt at worse to allow yet another miss opportunity for this country in search of a badly needed brake.

Let us get back to renewable energy. These Ideas are not far fetch nor impossible to realize. They are not fanciful nor utopian, but rather the necessary outcome of a rational, reason bound and logic driven class of people who see the world as having the capacity and the higher probability of peaceful development of nations in a world meant for humankind.

Thus when the American philosopher William James states and I quote:

"that Militarism is the sole nourisher of certain human virtue that the world can't let die, Until the peace party come up with a substitute for the disciplinary of war, their utopian goal is neither desirable nor practical"

One can forgive him for not having the foresight of the potential of science to answer some of the most vexing questions of our time and to provide such substitute to endless wars. Yes, such future is not only possible, it is within our grasp, all that is lacking is for the political and economic class to align their objective behind the science, the good science that has so far shown us the path through innumerable numbers of trials and errors, enormous human treasures.

Thus finally we can put to rest our hatred, greed, cynicism, racial prejudice, inertia, barbaric impulse to result to war as the instrument of plunder and arrive at peaceful coexistence as the only logical and reasonable path for humankind.

The alternative is the status quo of war for war's sake.

As William James put it in his short essay, the moral equivalent of war, he wrote: *History is a bath of blood. Greek history is a panorama of jingoism and imperialism. War for war's sake. Tails of how the Greeks glorified war and plunder permeates their history and it makes for terrible reading because of the horror of it all.* This history also tells us how the Greek went from the highest echelon of world civilization to utter ruin. Those wars were purely piratical, gold, slaves, women were the only motives.

Is this really the best we can do? We have spent the entire 20th century behaving more like the Greeks in their imperialist conquest. How is it that men of the modern world no longer sees the virtue of what was good from the Greeks. Fewer are those who still see Socrates, Plato, Aristotle as models but many are those who are clamoring for wars at the sight of the slightest disagreement on politics, social, economic and political discourse. We have wholeheartedly embraced this history of barbaric impulses of war for war's sake as we are getting further and further away from the intellectual know how of that époque. Truly if Williams James had live long enough to see ww2, Korea, Vietnam, iraq1 and iraq2,

Afghanistan, panama, Syria, Libya; he too would agreed that we have gone mad and have learned little from our past history. Modernity connote evolution, and evolution connote improvement from past failures.

Yes, we have evolved in many ways but at the same time our evolution is hostage to our epic failure to move away from wars as the first and only civilized solution in a world made of haves and have nots. Our progress is held hostage to thousands of nuclear warheads capable of destroying the world many times over. Our scientists are eager to put their science behind this collective mindset of destruction and not enough of them have used their moral authority born out of their superior knowledge to clamor for change. We have created a situation where the only outcome to prevent more catastrophic wars is for all nations to arms themselves with Nukes for only nuke is the guarantor of safety In This predatory world. Isn't this the definition of madness?

When will we ever reach a level of consciousness to facilitate dialogue and peaceful resolution of our differences? When will the scientific community push our leaders in that direction. Those brave scientists who still believe in the science for science's sake and not simply a tool to get rich at all cost should create a collective mindset in their line of work to put pressure on our leaders so that finally they can start to devise policies and laws fully aligned with the science.

The Higgs boson particle project at cern has finally close the loop on the long and arduous path science has followed since the days of Galileo Galilee and Copernicus who fathered the concept of heliocentrism, that the earth rotate around the sun daily and not the other way around. His ideas were vehemently opposed by the church who investigated the matter and concluded that heliocentrism was foolish and absurd since it contradicted holy scripture. He was put under house arrest until his death in 1642.

Where would we be today without Galileo and Copernicus scientific breakthroughs. Yes, it's true that we have made tremendous progress there too, for we no longer put scientists and philosophers to death for speaking the truth and for educating the world and helping mankind out of their inertia and ignorance, but what we do is equally devastating. Special interest spends billions of dollars to suffocate the good science with fully funded pseudo science. No where is this more prevalent then the oil and gas industry's efforts at silencing the science of global warming, while the military Coopt them into the science of destruction, where every discovery is put to the service of what Dwight Eisenhower called the military industrial complex. Eisenhower was highly perceptive for he also said and I quote: wars spend the dreams of our children and the geniuses of our brave scientists. He was so right on so many levels.

How many of our scientists are working on the next generation miniature nuclear warheads, or precision guided bombs, or predator drones to kill with impunity from 10,000 feet. How many young computer scientists are busy hacking adversaries both real and perceived, or busy devising the next secret virus to surreptitiously take over an adversary's computer system unaware, or worse virus to shot down civilian infrastructures energy pipelines, electric grids, airlines, all vulnerable to this state of perpetual war.

Don't take my word for it just pay attention to the real news these days and you see these things in the headlines but more importantly, for everyone of them big enough to make the six o'clock news there are dozen more undisclosed for various reasons, either for national security reasons as to not let the perpetrators know that they have succeeded, as is the case in Iran these days, which is under a barrage of attacks. Sometimes they report a fire, sometimes a press release announce a failed attempt. Then came the ransomeware attack on the colonial pipeline that shot down oil refineries from Texas all the way to the east coast.

Unfortunately, these kinds of acts will only intensify for as long as we refuse to obey the science that tells us we are all the same, just a multiplicity parts of the whole. The human genome project confirmed it at the gene and cellular level and the Large Hydra Collider (LHC) has confirmed it at the subatomic level, that we are all part of one continuum and it is time that we act like it.

IV

The Human Value Chain

We spend more than 15 years in school learning and after years of studying, we simply settle for a career. What about everything else that we were thought in school? Have they suddenly become irrelevant because you are making money and you have a career? I have heard all the time while I was in college and after I got out, people complaining why we have to learn all kind of subjects that we never get to use in real life. In my case, I studied, Latin and Greek and I too complained of the futility of these subjects as dead languages. It was not until later, as I begin to reach for broader knowledge that I realize how important and relevant these so called dead languages are to the contemporary world. As someone who speak several languages, I often reach back to Latin and Greek to decode a new word and with pinpoint accuracy, without having to pull a dictionary, I can find the meaning of new words by looking at their Latin or Greek origin.

This level of thinking exposes the real flaws of our education system that people equate a degree with an official seal of approval that they are educated and the only motivation for getting that degree or that seal of approval is to go out and make money. Teachers and professors did not spend countless hours teaching us critical thinking, philosophy, ethics, foreign language, science, geography, archeology, psychology, astrology, music, history, sociology only so that we can have our pick and ignore everything else.

A college degree only prepares you so that you can go and get the real education yourself. Of course, certain disciplines will take precedents over others base on what you like, dislike, and based on what you can do. Yes, you chose to be a layer, an accountant or Doctor but you should continue to learn everything else that your time permits. At a minimum, it will help you be better at your profession on so many levels but more importantly, it will guarantee your continuing evolution as a human being.

When we settle for soundbites and refuse to investigate the issue further, we are doing ourselves a disservice and society as a whole pays the consequences of our inconsequential actions. I cannot tell you how many times I was able to debunk a Facebook post, photo or story just by looking it up before I offer my comment. If I am able to do it so could everyone else and doing so, we will eventually play our role fully in helping those who are gullible enough to believe everything before checking it.

Whether it is a Nigerian Prince offering you a partnership in a scheme to bring diamond to the country. Whether it is your government who told you that they have to invade another country to bring democracy and safeguard human rights, you have a duty as citizen of the world to assume your responsibility and request more information to either support, debunk or resist based on your own judgement.

To that point a new class of journalists are required to search the truth zealously and bring it to the masses. The current for profit system of journalism is just another tool for the elite to obfuscate the truth and hide valid information from the masses.

We need investigative journalists like the occasional New York Times reports on specific issues of relevance, such as the Michael Brown shooting that led them to investigate the issue of police brutality further and in doing so was able to unmask the different tentacles of this problem for those willing to work toward a solution. We also have the Panama papers, another brilliant piece of investigatory work revealing the network of deceit by the elites to hide vast resources in different secret tax heaven to avoid paying taxes.

Moreover, these pieces need to reach the masses so that they can form a better opinion of the realities of this world and create a balance in their lives between entertainments, sports, social media and the need to evolve, and for life itself is a journey towards a better self.

I grew up in a large family. Growing up in Haiti, we were not rich by US standard but we counted in the top 10 % in the country in terms of living standard, which was not much. It only meant that we had a descent home, a vacation house in the countryside, private car, a small business that dad ran and occasional trip to NY for some of my brothers and we had a lot of our extended family in US as a backup should things get tough.

Our parent always reinforced in all of us certain ethics and morals about life in general. We knew that we were somewhat privileged simply by looking at living conditions of the population. They thought us to always appreciate what we have and to always share with each other first and to whom ever is in need regardless if it's an extended family, a friend or a total stranger.

I could remember many instances when dad's brothers bailed him out. First, his brothers when his small business failed, arrested, and forced into exile by the dictator who ran the country for 14 years. It was his brothers who got him out of the country and helped him settle in NY.

We learned the importance of sharing and giving and helping others because we had been in the receiving end of that noble life principal more than once.

This is the legacy of our family and I must say, it is part of our culture. Families take care of each other no matter what, some are better at it then others but it is this practice that has enable the country to go through all the hardships.

Whether it is back-to-back hurricanes or earthquake or flood, Haiti still stands strong, its sons and daughters in the diaspora, no matter where they are or how long they have left the country, never really renounce their identity, they never forget those left behind. According to recent World Bank estimate, the Haitian Diaspora sends on average more than $1.8 billion dollars in remittances to Haiti.

Thanks to this culture of goodwill, millions of Haitians are kept alive, with enough to eat and some to send their kids to school. However, evolution requires better conditions then bare survival. Haiti, like all other third world countries, need quality education, quality healthcare, good paying jobs, modern infrastructure and security. These are the necessary conditions for people to evolve.

Whenever people ask me, where are you from? I proudly answer Haiti. I usually get all kinds of reactions, some are shocked because in their mind, there is a stereotypical view of what a Haitian look or sounds like and I do not fit the stereotype, others sometimes shows empathy for the well-known hardship and poverty and still others do not even know where Haiti is. However, usually, no one seems to know anything else beyond the fact that the country is poor or unlucky. No one knows, why or how, when the how and why is facing them every day, in the global economic structure of our current system, which allows a few rich and powerful countries to claim the vast majority of the world resources to the detriment of vast majority.

It is almost with pleasure that I speak to every one of them according to their understanding of Haiti. To some I have to inform them that every country on earth has three classes of people in it evolving at any given time, rich, middle class and poor. The only difference is the percentage of each class depending on the country.

In some country with greater wealth and resources, the percentage of poor people tend to be smaller but still they have poor people just like any other country. I usually take the example of the US and say, to assume that all Haitians are poor, illiterate, and tantamount to me saying that the living conditions of millions of people in the ghettos or rural America are a complete representation of the American reality.

Of course, that is false and an ignorant position or assumption, but yet, I am amazed at the number of well-meaning and educated people who holds such view of Haiti and the Haitian people.

After I graduated from college, I made it a point to continue to learn everything there is to learn about life. A great deal of that learning comes from been an active observer of the world. It is part of my process of learning, along with reading and talking to people. I had developed a routine that I believe worked well for me. It is my ability to think freely and reason as a process of understanding the information that I am absorbing. I therefore like to question everything until it make sense before I absorb it as truth and therefore a principal worth incorporating in my day to day life.

As a born again Christian, I watched, as all of this became an impediment to my faith. To practice the faith, I could not question anything in the Bible. I could not even rely on my own logic and ability to understand what I was reading.

My whole life I have carefully navigated from country to country, childhood to maturity and from culture to culture relying always on my ability to understand everything around me. I went from a baby with no sense of the world, to learning to speak four languages, mathematics, biology, sociology, philosophy, geography, history, physics and chemistry (although I was not great in the last two). Why is it that only the bible requires special skills not of this world to understand it? Life and the observable reality is made of a set of understandable truths.

That is what reality is. A set of commonly agreed principles and truths that govern all of our actions. For example, to know that if I run across the street in front of a moving car I might get hit. If I jump off a building, I will get hurt and possibly die. If I am hungry, it means I need to eat. If I am tired, it means I need to rest. If I want to know something, it means that i need to learn it. The same is true for religious concepts. Asking people to give up their ability to reason and think as a condition to know God is counterproductive, for these are the very tools that have carried men from his caves to the stars.

When we apply reason and logic as the guiding principles for our daily interaction with the world, a set of common beauty emerges. Here, we mean by beauty all that is in sync with life, the sun rising in the morning, the stars that shine above our heads at night, the flowers that bloom, the cities we built, the technologies we use, the food that grows from the ground with just water and sunlight.

Moreover, logic and reason also reveals indisputable truths to us, if we are curious enough to search for them. One of these truths is the human value chain.

Our true value as human being is the total sum of the value of the planet divided by the number of citizens living on it at any given time. The total value of the earth is continually increasing exponentially with each discovery such as the Bronze Age had a value, the renaissance age another, and the industrial age yet another value. Each one exponentially higher than the other, because, each represent an époque in human evolution where new knowledge, new information is released.

With each leap forward, the knowledge gain opens the door to even more knowledge, which, collectively serve to create the world that we live in today.

The total sum of the value of the earth is comprised of everything in it, including silver, copper, diamond, rubies, oil, rare earth, natural gas, all the wealth contain in and beneath the sea. Moreover, everything that we collectively discover on earth in the future, as well as in space that increases the total value of the wealth on earth, belongs to the same pool. Why, you would ask, should Russia, China and America share any wealth found on mars or the moon with any other nations. The answer is simply because they used our collective resources, the common wealth of the planet, to reach Mars and the moon or any other stars or planet.

The elements of the earth, is what is capable of transforming the raw materials of the planet into spaceships, or Hubble telescope or the international space stations or the technology used to such use.

This is not only logical and truth, but known in the elite circle. Why else, would they create a system to brain wash the masses to submission, while they are busy unlocking the secrets of the earth, in search of eternal life here on earth.

Each time there is a great new discovery, the value of the citizen on earth increases commensurately.

I recently watched a Utube video by Lynette Zang, titled "the Currency Reset", dated August 29, 2020. She is the Chief Market Analyst at ITM Trading. In that educational video, Lynette shared with the public a series of financial data points that help me better understand the hidden treasures of the planet and how the elites are plundering it.

Lynette Zang estimates, the total sum of collaterized debt globally is somewhere in the neighborhood of $460 Trillion dollars. This sum includes all countries and all other forms of debts, bond, treasury, mortgage, college, credit card, corporate, etc...

This discovery also applies to the field of science and technology for nothing discovered is the sole proprietor of the discoverer. It is like saying a stranger comes to my house and found a rare painting in the attic that I did not know was there and he or she claims it as his or hers because I did not know it was there. The law in any country would find such a claim to be without merit. The same is true for any discovery made by any human being on earth at any given time in the past or the future.

Not all of this negates the fact that those on the upper echelon of society do not deserve a life commensurate to their duties and responsibilities.

A farmer in Wisconsin or Ohio does not need to have a private jet and several homes in different continent but it is acceptable for the head of Microsoft or any global company to have access to such things.

Only because it is necessary to perform his or her duties. Beyond that, the idea that one man can be worth the combine value of millions of people and lay claim to that wealth as his personal wealth because he or she had an idea that made it possible for him or her to build that kind of wealth is fanciful.

I therefore say, please show me an idea that someone had and developed it into a multibillion dollar enterprise by himself or herself and without using any of the raw materials on earth. Show me that person and I will say only he or she has a claim to that wealth, but such person does not exist yet. Only God or the creator can lay such a claim for it is after all he who made all of this possible and perhaps has a plan for humankind that is unknown to us all. Beyond that, Billionaires and multibillion dollar companies are simply managers of our wealth and should use it for the collective well being.

After every American or French or Chinese citizens have access to quality education, quality healthcare, affordable housing, adequate food security and proper infrastructure for their respective society to function it is then a requirement that the extra wealth be redistributed to those countries with limited resources and wealth to help create the same conditions for everyone on earth.

Wealth inequality will always exist but at an acceptable level.

When society create a set of conditions that lock you in a routine for your entire short existence, then you simply can never grow. You simply cannot evolve.

The right conditions for human evolution requires that you have access to basic needs such as food, healthcare, housing and education. Once you are able to meet these needs, you can devote more time to leisure and further educate yourself about things that matter in this world, like how many planets are there in our solar system and what exist beyond these nine planets.

Where life does come from? What is the law of nature that Einstein theorized about that to every action there is an equal and opposite reaction? These are existential questions that one must continuously strive to understand; rather than wasting your precious times in fruitless exercises.

I am not a religious bigot, I am just one who sees the 'I" as essential to who "I" am and therefore, want to do all possible to understand these things.

People who are locked in a continuous struggle just to survive daily with less than $1/day, cannot even begin to contemplate these vexing questions about life, existence and our place in the universe.

Evolution requires constant learning, constant challenge. Learning can take all forms. Meeting new people is learning, moving to a new job is learning. Moving to a different neighborhood is learning. Go to a different restaurant from time to time is learning, change the conversation around the dinner table from time to time is more opportunity for learning.

Let kids have a voice and lead the conversations at the dinner table from time to time is also learning for their generation is different than yours and therefore, their experience is exponentially different than yours.

Go to a different country each vacation is learning and especially avoid all-inclusive hotels where you go from an inclusive environment to fly hundreds of miles away to a new country with a vibrant people, culture, food, language etc...

If you are going to stay at an all-inclusive hotel, the least you can do is to take one or two days to venture out into the country to see the people and interact with them.

Learning something new, every opportunity you have for as long as you can is the natural process of evolution. Malcolm Gladwell in his famous book, "outliers" through meticulous investigatory work, he discovers that human needs on average 10,000 hours to master anything. To be a true expert at everything.

Ten thousand hours is essentially the equivalent of 10 years, what then do you do with the rest of your time on earth once you have mastered a specific field or skill. You spend the rest of your time making money with that skill as if Money is the ultimate prize. It is good to have money even better to know you will never run out of it but it can not be your raison d'être. Money should only be the means to an end and that the end itself.

This is the problem with today's scientists and inventors, they are capitalist first and a scientist second, meaning, if the idea is not marketable, capable of yielding huge profit, they do not pursue it, even if it has the potential to expand human life by a few decades.

Back to my favorite Billionaire, Elon Musk. For what I have read, the man is a gifted genius destined to solve many of the world's problems.

I have read his path from his childhood in South Africa to his first migration to Canada and then on to the US. His voracious appetite for reading. I was impressed to read that he once read all the books in his school's library. I admire his unique ability to overcome physical, mental and psychological obstacles, skills without which he could not have achieved this level of success. His work ethics, working tirelessly all hours of day and night to start his first company, Zip2.

However, I can not comprehend the fact that despite his enormous success and his early experience of the system of oppression that existed in his homeland, South Africa. The man, the visionary, the problem solver has not invested part of his wealth to the one problem that should have marked and helped to shape his earliest understanding of the world. Despite his earliest experience, as someone who has lived and experienced apartheid that the man who dreamed of sending us to the moon and to colonize mars and other planets someday, have yet to turn his ingenuity to this much closer at home problem in South Africa.

It baffles me even further knowing that his field of expertise and investments, namely technology, computer science and transportation are all areas South Africa lacks significantly and black south Africans in particular, as a direct result of the system of apartheid.

How does he not see the need to address this much closer to home problem, and a lot easier to rectify. Has he invested in a few STEM programs (science, technology, Engineering and Math). Such an investment could have helped to bridge the gap between white and black South Africans, and prepare a new generation of South Africans to eventually join his many companies. How many black South Africans are working for him at many of these companies. Has he used his enormous wealth and some of his inventions to help bring electricity to the poor town of Soweto, South Africa and other towns like it. I hope I am wrong that he has indeed done these things but I have not yet seen the evidence. (Note: after writing this chapter, I have read recently, that Musk Intends to donate a vast sum to help the UN fight hunger and to different charities), to which I say, kudos but I equally say, it is not donation, nor charity. It is just wealth redistribution and if it is well intended should go to fix real problems, like building g schools, roads, hospitals, clinics, teaching farmers how to grow more food and giving them the proper tools to do it and building the right infrastructure to help these products to market. This is the kind of investments that are needed in parts of the world with the greatest needs.)

So far, the so called world of philanthropy, charity is just that, charity design to keep the recipient in their current state and not design to fix poverty or hunger or illiteracy etc...

This is the dichotomy I see even in the few well-meaning billionaires and let's face it, there are not too many of them.

I admire Elon's hard work and success and join him in his quest to solve these problems but for heaven's sake, why can't any of these guys see what I am seeing, that our planet earth is the only home we have and it can't be safe until we are all safe. You can solve the energy crisis, you might even colonize mars, but you still need earth to replenish, food, oxygen, medicine, fuel and everything else human needs to survive.

Elon's fortune and career mark one of the greatest and most inspiring story of our generation. Burst into the scene at an early age and built several successful companies, from Zip2 to X.com, to Paypal, to Space X, Tesla and Solar City. The man is indeed a genius but all of his success and others like him is due to a simple truth: that it is the elements of the earth plus the energy of his employees that have helped to materialize each one of these companies.

Companies must exist to solve problems and when a company reach this level of success, it has a duty to reach those less fortunate on the planet to help alleviate their suffering. These are not philanthropies or humanitarian aid, it is properly called, wealth redistribution in the form of dividend to those that are in need.

The alternative is what we currently have, a world divided into 3 tiers, first, second and third world. Yet, science tells us that we all leave in one echo system, where everything is connected. What we do in one world has infinite consequences in the other parts of the world. For example, you can not solve the problem of global warming by providing renewable energy to the first world and disregard the rest of the world. It will not work. You have to address it all.

Of course, it is not easy and yes, it is a highly complex situation, but where we are genuine in our approach, that ought to be the goal, the objective. The Wright brothers did not take flight on their first try, and they did not go from single engine airplanes to supersonic technology overnight. It took countless trials and errors and continuous efforts to perfect the knowledge gained. Why then, do we not apply the same emergency, the same ethic behind these vexing issues of our time, namely the environment, the mountains of trash all over the planet and the ocean, illiteracy, famine, sickness and diseases across the world.

All we seem able to do is carve out a small piece of heaven for a small minority to experience life, all the while, billions continue to live in hell on earth. Moreover, their hell is the reason why our paradise will not last, for what is happening in their world will impact our paradise and inversely so.

The Ethical use of Social Media as a tool for change

L ike many things in life, social media platforms can be a double edge sword. On the one hand, it can be a tool for social reengineering, mind control and manipulation. We find evidence of this throughout these platforms. A proliferation of hate speech, propaganda, falsehood, lies to promote specific nefarious agendas, be it political, economic, social or religious. We also find evidence of this nefarious use of these platforms in the proliferation of obscenities, of all kinds, the wasting of precious time in promoting gossips of all kinds.

Having said that, responsible people of all back grounds can find in these platforms a portal for promoting good ideas, progressive ideas, socially constructive ideas capable of helping to build a better future for all.

To illustrate my point, I compile a list of examples where social media platforms like face book, Tik tok, Instagram, twitter and others, have plaid a major role in promoting justice and peace for the voiceless and marginalized people all across the globe.

A prominent example of this is the Arab spring of 2010 that led a massive movement for social change across the Arab world, leading to the destitution of several governments. Another prominent example of this is the Black lives matter movement, right before the pandemic. While the "BLM" movement has since been discredited, its impact on bringing police brutality to millions of living rooms in America has left an indelible taste in the national psyche, that after all, black people were not inventing these injustices. They are the everyday reality of too many black and brown people across the land.

We look at the last few years and we see an increasing number of young black and brown people shot by cops not in self-defense, but almost casually. There was the claim that Michael brown charged on the cop who shot him. Then you have Eric Gardner in Staten Island and so on. Between 2014 and 2019, 1,653 black people died at the hands of US police. Here is a short list of police shootings, according to Al Jazeera publication and almost every one of them were the result of single individual with nothing else but a cell phone and access to one of these social media platforms. In some cases broadcasted live for the world to see:

Rayshard Brooks, 27 years old

Rayshard was the victim of police shooting in Atlanta Georgia. He fell asleep in his car, blocking the drive-through lane of wendy's restaurant. The police cameras showed that for officers Garrett Rolfe and Devin Brosnan speaking to Rayshard for more than 40 minutes. The police told him he had too much to drink and they tried to arrest him. He fled and was shot twice in the back.

Daniel Prude, 41

Daniel was shot in Rochester New York. He had run into the street naked while experiencing a mental breakdown, health episode. He was initially compliant after the emergency services found him at 3:00 Am.

He became agitated and police placed a spit hood on his head. Officer Mark Vaughn used his body weight to force Prude's head against the pavement, as others restrained him. He was restrained in that position for over 3 minutes. An autopsy found that Prude died of complications of asphyxia due to the restraint, as well as acute intoxication.

George Floyd, 46

George floyd's death was broadcasted on live television for the world to see, which sparked a global response against police treatment of black and brown people all over the world. George was killed in Minneapolis, Minnesota, for allegedly trying to use a $20 counterfeit bill. Floyd was handcuffed on the ground as officer Derek Chauvin Knelt on his neck for eight minutes and 46 seconds. He complained to the four officers that he could not breath and became unresponsive. Two autopsy reports listed Floyd's death as homicide, although they gave different causes.

Breonna Taylor, 26

Breonna was killed in Louisville Kentucky, while sleeping in her own home. Her and her boyfriend, Kenneth Walker, were sleeping when three plainclothes officers arrived at their apartment to execute a search warrant in a drug case. They believed it was a break-in and walker called 911 and fired his licensed firearm. Taylor who was unarmed was shot eight times.

Ataliana Jefferson, 28

Ataliana was killed in Miami Florida. Police officer shot and killed her through the window of her home, in the presence of her eight-year-old nephew. The police were responding to a call from a neighbor who reported that Jefferson's front window had been left open.

Aura Rosser, 40

Aura was killed in Ann Arbor, Michigan, at home. Her boyfriend called police to ask them to escort her out of the house because of an altercation. The official report says that she was holding a knife when the police arrived. Officer Mark Raab used his Taser. Officer David Reid fired a single shot that killed her.

Stephon Clark, 22

Stephon was killed in 2018 in Sacramento California, standing in his grand mother's back yard. Officers said they believe he was holding a gun as they shot at him more than 20 times. Clarke was only holding a mobile phone.

Botham Jean, 26

Botham was killed in 2018 in Dallas Texas seated on his sofa at home eating ice scream. He was shot by an off-duty police officer, Amber Guyger after she entered his apartment believing, she said that it was hers and he was a dangerous intruder.

Philando Castille, 32

Castille was killed in 2016 over a routine traffic stop. Police video of the stop shows a police officer shooting Castille seconds after he informed him that he had a legal firearm. Castille girlfriend, Diamond Reynolds, who was in the car, along with her four years old daughter, captured the aftermath on facebook live.

Alton Sterling, 37

Alton was killed in 2016 in Baton Rouge Louisiana. He was selling CDs and DVDs. He was shot by officer Blane Salamoni, one of the two officers who confronted Alton outside a shop. He was tasered and pinned to the ground before being shot six times. In video footage, Salamoni can be heard traetening to shoot Sterling in the head.

Michelle Cusseaux, 50

Michelle was killed in 2015 while at home in Phoenix Arizona. Four officers arrived to serve a court ordered transport to an impatient mental health facility. Possibly confused, Cusseaux had an exchange with the officers, who decided to remove her security door. They said she charged towards them with a hammer. Sergeant Percy Dupra fired a single shot and she died shortly thereafter.

Freddie Gray, 25

Freddie died in 2015 in a police van. Gray had been arrested and placed in the back of a police van. He was found dead 45 minutes later, his spinal cord nearly severed. His hands and feet had been shackled and without a seatbelt, he could not protect himself as he was tossed around inside the vehicle.

Fanisha Fonville, 20

Fanisha died in 2015 at home in Charlotte, North Carolina. Officer Anthony Holzhauer and Shon Sheffield answered a distress call to take Fonville to a mental health facility. According to Fonville's partner Korneshia banks, Fonville had a knife and she was worried that she might hurt herself. Officer Holzhauer shot Funville. The official account says Fonville lunged at the officers with a knife. Banks says she did not see a knife in Fonville's hand when she was shot.

Eric Garner, 43

Eric was killed in 2014 allegedly selling loose cigarettes in Staten Island, NY. Officer Daniel Pantaleo held Eric in a chokehold that he did not release in spite of Garner saying" I cant breath" 11 times.

Akai Gurley, 28

Akai died in 2014 in Brooklyn, NY walking down the stairs in the building where he lived. Police officer Peter Liang and his partner were conducting a vertical patrol in a housing project. Liang entered an unlit stairwell, and fired his weapon. The bullet bounced off a wall and killed Gurley.

Tamir Rice, 12

Tamir was killed in Cleveland Ohio, while playing with a toy gun in a park. Within two seconds of arriving at the park, officer Timothy Loehmann had fatally shot Rice. Police then talked his 14 year old sister, Tajai, to the ground, handcuffed her in the back of a police car. It took four minutes for officers to administer first aid to Rice. He died in hospital the following day.

Michael Brown, 18

Michael was killed in 2014, in Ferguson Missouri while walking with a friend. A white police officer confronted brown with his friend. A scuffle ensued and the officer, Darren Wilson – shot and killed brown, Wilson said he acted in self-defense.

Tanisha Anderson, 37

Tanisha died in Cleveland Ohio, in 2014. Here family called 911 for help because Tanisha, who was bypolar, was restless and trying to leave the house. Investigators estimates that she was handcuffed to the ground for 21 minutes before paramedics arrived.

Also not on this list but equally relevant are these 3 police shootings of Amadou Diallo with 41 bullets in Brooklyn NY, in 1999, Trevon Martin in Florida in 2012 by a neighborhood watchman, George Zimmerman and Abner Louima who was sexually sodomized in 1997 in the bathroom of a police station in NY after he was arrested outside a Brooklyn nightclub.

Sources of the list of victims of police shootings, Aljezeera by interactive. aljazeera.com and by Alia Chught

Where logic and reason dictate human behavior, a different set of outcome is possible, by that I mean, the concept of reasonable force proportionate to the threat. Logic and reason would propel anyone who is about to take a life, to ask these rhetorical questions. Is this right, am I in self defensive mode, thus protecting my very person, or am I about to kill someone because I am unable to restrain myself. Is the accused, or presumed accused a threat to me or to others? If yes, deadly force is reasonable in preventing a larger crime from taking place. If the presumed accused running away from me, he or she is not armed and the crime itself is petty in nature, a small robbery, a counterfeit currency, a street vendor of cigarettes, breaking nuisance laws, a broken taillight, a red light. Is deadly force reasonable in these circumstances. Logic and reason would conclude, no.

There are plenty of police officers who have retired with honor and never discharged their weapons once. I know, because I have two such officers in my family. I have two cousins that retired from the New York City Policy force, after many decades of service. During their career, they received many promotions, all the way to sergeant. One of them served in the security details of the New York city Mayor. The other retired early and continues to lend his service to the United Nations peace keeping forces, helping and sharing his expertise in the formation of new police officers in various under developed countries, including his native land, Haiti. It is true these UN missions in Haiti have failed in many ways then one, but such failure can not be attributed to him. To the contrary, the means by which I measure his success is in the number of new recruits he was able to train. One can only hope that those new officers are now serving with distinctions like he did during his career.

The failure of the UN missions to Haiti is part of a bigger problem, that we find mostly in the third world. It is often referred to as the ruled based international order, something the French President likes to refer to from time to time. The rules based international order is a system that allows rich and powerful countries to oppress smaller and weaker states for their economic gain. It has been so for thousands of years and despite our higher state of consciousness, in the present, brought about by our scientific achievements in many areas, we seem unable to build a better society, one that allows itself to be lead by logic and reason and back by the scientific knowledge we have gained over the last century.

I share the story of my two cousins with you as a way to illustrate a larger point. That there are ways to be a force for good, in any profession, even in one such as law enforcement, where one is more prone to violence. This issue goes to the state of mind. No one is born with the capacity to self awareness and able to discern and manage one's emotions. Such capacity is gained over time with continuing efforts to elevate oneself above the pettiness of every day living.

When you are able to manage your emotion at that level, a set of common beauties emerge, the beauty we find in peaceful coexistence, in empathizing with the pain and suffering of the other.

Reason and logic are those principles that will get you to that state of mind. The state of mind that allows one to rise above the pettiness in life, above all these negative emotions that unfortunately, our society thrives upon. Once, you are there, you will find a sense of clam, peace and serenity, a sense of oneness. The kind that one can only assume comes from being truly one with the body, soul and spirit, where the three entities are moving through life in sync with each other.

Eventually, you will be able to compare and contrast your state of mind with the daily realities around you, not for boastful purposes but simply for further self edification. You will find the true nature of the world we live in is one that is in dire need of self correction, self amelioration and you will indelibly reach the same conclusion as I did, that evolution, true evolution is all around us and it is constant. We see evidence of this throughout the cosmos. We look at science which tells us that stars are born and have a shelf life, commensurate with the amount of hydrogen and helium they consume and based on the rate of consumption. When the helium and hydrogen run out, the star either explodes or collapses on itself in a process scientists call supernova or pulsar. That explosion itself is not without reason.

It takes billions of years for stars and planets to form and reform all in a constant search of something greater. Our solar system is born out of that same process, we call creation. We can only conclude from the mechanics that govern our solar system that once such intelligence is gained, it is to be maintained and protected for all time and any tweaking to it is to gain more intelligence, or to perfect it even further. It is never to be destroyed or disregarded. The intelligence behind our solar system is not without an equally genius architect. Religion calls it God, but for scientists, Atheist, or agnostics, such intelligence is without question the reason we are all here. Moreover, our knowledge of the cosmos is infinitely smaller than what we still don't know and that in of itself ought to give us pose in what we do and how we live our life.

The intelligence behind our solar system and indeed throughout the cosmos is no different then the logic and reason of which I am speaking of. Such intelligence is in us. We are indeed a unique species born out of this process of evolution. Our planet earth is also unique and precious as we are, and plays a central role in our very existence. Thus taking care of it is as paramount as anything else we do, for it is that which allows us to evolve and gain further knowledge of ourselves and of the cosmos. Thus, we are inexorably lead to conclude that of all the human attributes, logic and reason are those main attributes that should dictate human actions and interactions with each other and with its surroundings. Logic and reason are those attributes that open doors to greater wisdom, thus greater knowledge for our continuing evolution, as perhaps it was intended.

VI

The more things appear to change the more they stay the same

In 2004, my job transferred me to Bermuda where I worked for more than 10 years.

It is August 2010, another beautiful Monday in Bermuda. I decided to walk to the office, so that I could listen to my morning music, but I also needed to prepare mentally for a secret meeting with the head of insurance operations for ESL Insurance, one of our biggest trading partner.

She is an older woman in her mid-60s. She has been in the industry long before I started. I first met her in NY when she headed the healthcare insurance operation for Employer's Reinsurance Corporation (ERC), a subsidiary of General Electric (GE).

I got in the office early, reviewed the file that I would present to her. It is a proposal for a new product with the potential to revolutionize the Bermuda marketplace. The product was the hard work of 2 years of negotiations with all the stakeholders in the marketplace, as many as 12 insurance companies. We engaged with their respective general counsels to create a new insurance policy and reinsurance certificate to address a number of lingering issues in the marketplace. These two policies provided clients with contract certainty, allowing them to buy as much insurance as needed with as many insurance partners under one contract.

My team included my general counsel and my team's vice president at the time. While waiting for her, I sip on a fresh cup of coffee and entered in casual talks with my teammates. She came in a few minutes later and in the course of casual introduction, somehow we ended up talking about her new house recently built in Wilmington, North Carolina. Apparently, a beautiful house on the coast. She primarily wanted us to know this because her husband, an avid fisherman who also owns a boat in Bermuda, was about to buy a new fishing boat for the new house, something she thought would sheer us up, since some of us go out fishing with her husband occasionally.

This is how I came to know of a town name Wilmington, in North Carolina. Prior to that conversation, my knowledge of the state was limited to the cities of Charlottesville, Ashville, Cary and Raleigh, 4 beautiful cities where we had corporate offices and that I had a few hospital clients, including the largest health system in the state.

While looking at different documentaries on the issue of police conduct, brought about by the string of police shootings in the last few years, I stumbled on the 1898 massacre in Wilmington. This came about from a casual conversation with my young cousin who is a public school teacher. He and I exchange ideas from time to time about the ongoing issues with the election, and most recently the January 6th, insurrection. He exclaimed, that the more things appear to change the more they stay the same, because the invasion on January 6th, is nothing compare to what did happen in 1898, in Wilmington, North Carolina. I did not know what my cousin was talking about so, I asked him for details and this is how I came to know about long forgotten history of the massacre in Wilmington North Carolina, in 1898.

The 1898 massacre in Wilmington, NC, happened because the town republicans at the time became very diverse with several prominent black elected politicians in various positions. The town also saw a growing and affluent black middle class of prominent lawyers, doctors, teachers and professors and nurses.

The Democrats at the time were on the side of the white ruling class, this was before the southern strategy that saw republicans appealed to white racial grievances to gain their support. Prior to that, most blacks were republicans.

The White ruling class in North Carolina declared that this is their country and they would not submit to Negro rules. They orchestrated a coup that eventually striped the blacks of political power. That was not enough, because blacks continue to maintain a respectable position economically in the town. These white mobs, then proceeded to kill and burn down several black owned businesses, including a black own newspaper. More than 2,100 blacks fled to nearby cemetery, and forest and bushes where they hid for days in the cold rain.

Eventually, many more blacks fled the town, reducing their number from 126,000 registered voters prior to the massacre to just above 6,000 decades later. It took another 90 years before the town elected another black to political office. The massacre had achieved two objectives, deplete black people of any access to economic independence and limit or eliminate their voting rights. It just so happened that these are the very same rights enshrined in the declaration of independence and the bill of rights. Thus one wonder, were these rights intended to build a more equitable society, or were they just a mirage for the purpose of projecting a semblance of a unique multi racial democracy, the likes of which the world has never seen. Such a society could have been and still could be a true beacon of hope for humanity. A true beacon of hope for humanity. Unfortunately, we now know too well, that such an objectif, has yet to be realized and our current course, seems to indicate that we are far from achieving it, unless God intervene.

For more information on this event, I refer you to this book: Wilmington's Lie, written by journalist and pulitzerPrize-winning journalist, David Zucchino.

Tulsa Oklohoma,

Just 23 years later after the Wilmington massacre, another event reminds us of this dichotomy, this dissonance, between what we say and what we actually do. This time it is in Tulsa Oklohoma, about 1,200 miles away, crossing the states of Tennessee and Arkansas.

The year is 1921 in Tulsa Oklahoma. Another town with another growing black middle class massacred by a white mob. In a neighborhood called the Greenwood district, with a vibrant business district known as "Black Wall Street". An old time downtown with dozens of black owned business, like movie theaters, pharmacies, stores, etc..

On May 30, 1921, a 19-year-old shoeshine Blackman name Dick Rowland had an ill-fated encounter with a 17-year-old white girl elevator operator name Sarah Page in the Drexel Building. The girl screamed and they both ran outside the building. No one knows what exactly happened but a day later Dick Rowland was arrested, they claimed that Dick Rowland had assaulted Sarah. In the courthouse, hundreds of white people descended on black Wall Street, armed. Whites outnumbered the black residents. They fought back but were overrun by the white mob. They burned down the district and killed their way through. The exact number of casualties are hard to confirm, because to this day, the bodies were never recovered. More than 1,200 buildings burned in an area of 35 square blocks.

There are a lot more examples of similar events throughout history. We could for example list the many examples where a formal agreement is reached; documents are signed and agreed by two parties only to be discarded once they get what they want. This is how the Haitian revolutionary leader, Toussaint Louverture was captured by the French troops, after they promised him to retire with honor. Toussaint was a former slave who led a successful slave revolt. He eventually became governor general of the island under the control of Napoleon. Toussaint wanted to keep the former slaves free but did not want to part ways with France. Realizing Toussaint brilliance as a military tactician, the French devised a plot to seize him. He was offered to retire with honor and convinced to lay down his arms in return for Napoleon not to reinstate slavery.

A few weeks later, he was invited to a parley by a French general. Toussaint was seized at the French general's home and sent to fort de joux where he was confined and interrogated repeatedly and where he died in April 1803.

Following Toussaint's arrest, his second in command, General Jean Jacques Dessalines, realized there is no negotiating with the opposition and went on all-out war to the end. Haiti won that war and declared its independence from France in November 18, 1803. Dessalines became the country's first Emperor.

Another similar example, this time among themselves. The same trick applied during World War II, between Adolph Hitler and Stalin in the biggest double cross ever, known as Operation Barbarosa. The Germans fed Stalin lies after lies promising to be ally and not to invade Russia, all the while millions of German troop's line up the front line. Stalin did not believe the British multiple attempts to warn them that Germany was about to attack. Eventually the attack came and Stalin was not prepared. Stalin eventually prevailed but only after being bailed out by the winter temperature that rendered the battlefield impractical. Here I offer only a summary of the event, because it is just anecdotal evidence of a much bigger problem that permeates our society, our culture.

In a world where nothing on the surface is what it seems, where lies, better lies, deception and obfuscation seem to be the main currency, one must try to reach out to likeminded people of all background, race, ethnicity, religion or class to help spark a greater light into this world.

You see, hardship, adversity and difficulties in life are all there to remind you from time to time to refocus the mind on what matters most, unfortunately, those at the top of the system have used these adversities and difficult moments in life to rob you of that life, by creating more obstacles to prevent you from reaching your full potential.

Until such time that God makes his grand entrance to claim paternity of all this as his and make known his plan for mankind, our only choice, is to thrive to elevate reason and logic as our guiding principles for a better world. Take what is yours not through malice, lies, deception, unethical behaviors, but simply by applying yourself at every situation, every encounter, to simply be a force for good.

God will act in his time, I do not know when or how, but we know that science has yet to answer this vexing question about the existence of the universe and how it came to be. Their theories do offer some clues. I know this because when I look at the data available to all of us, I see a solar system made of the Sun and nine planets moving in circular motion around the sun.

I see of the nine planets only one is capable of sustaining life in all its forms. Only one is capable of providing the necessary conditions to not only live, but to exist by providing all that is needed to create new conditions to fully experience life, in creating, innovating, solving problems, all the while learning all there is to learn to evolve into a better self. I also see and understand that within our solar system, exist the Kuiper belt, which encircles our solar system in the form of a protective shield.

The French philosopher, Pascal Blaise, once said and I quote "Science without a conscience is a recipe for disaster".

Knowledge without virtue can lead men to its destruction.

Wisdom is the difference between those who are able to use their knowledge to serve their barbaric impulses, and those who are able to use their knowledge for the good of humanity, by creating better conditions for humanity to experience life.

Reason is that force, which propels us towards the divine. Many philosophers have shared this perspective with us throughout the ages. For these philosophers, to live in the light, is to be guided by reason and when you are guided by reason, your knowledge becomes an intuitive force for good.

Let us take for example the effect of Fire. It is one of rare materials on earth that is able to multiply when you divide it. With a single candle light, you are able to light many other candles, without reducing the flame from the original candle. It is idem for knowledge, when you share your knowledge with others, you do not lose that knowledge. Unlike money, if you have a million dollars and you donate half of it to charity, or a friend in need, it is still an act of kindness, but the fact remains that you no longer have a million dollars. If you share your knowledge with others, you do not lose that which you know, in fact you reinforce it.

Rare are those scientists who are still committed to science for science's sake and advocate for a culture that follows the science and uses it for the good of humanity, better conditions, healthy conditions. We know, too well, what is hailing our society, with sickness and diseases, with contaminated food supply and water supply, yet, we do very little to address these vexing conditions because, doing so means diverting resources from economic growth for the sake of creating more billionaires then to create better conditions for all to evolve.

Lastly, I advise you to read Plato's Allegory, copy of which is included in the Index section. Even, if you are familiar with it, or have read it a long time ago, just take a minute and read it immediately after you have read this book. You will finally understand that Plato was not just a philosopher, but a visionary.

Book VII, Allegory, is the most accurate reflection of our contemporary state, as a civilization and Plato described it in such details, not even the prophet Isaiah or Daniel of the ancient testament had such insight into the things of the future. His essential point is that most of us are puppet easily manipulated by the system but he also offers a way out to freedom. That those who seek to use logic and reason instead of fear and love of the cravings of the senses, can find the path to freedom. This book is but one more piece to the puzzle for those who seek this path.

Plato's The Republic, Book VII

THE ALLEGORY OF THE CAVE

SOCRATES: Next, said I [= Socrates], compare our nature in respect of education and its lack to such an experience as this.

PART ONE:

SETTING THE SCENE: THE CAVE AND THE FIRE

The cave
SOCRATES: Imagine this: People live under the earth in a cave like dwelling. Stretching a long wayup toward the daylight is its entrance, toward which the entire cave is gathered. The people have been inthis dwelling since childhood, shackled by the legs and neck..Thus they stay in the same place so that there is only one thing for them to look that: whatever they encounter in front of their faces. But because they areshackled, they are unable to turn their heads around.

A fire is behind them, and there is a wall between the fire and the prisoners
SOCRATES: Some light, of course, is allowed them, namely from a fire that casts its glow towardthem from behind them, being above and at some distance. Between the fire and those who are shackled[i.e., behind their backs] there runs a walkway at a certain height. Imagine that a low

wall has been builtthe length of the walkway, like the low curtain that puppeteers put up, over which they show their puppets.

The images carried before the fire
SOCRATES: So now imagine that all along this low wall people are carrying all sorts of things thatreach up higher than the wall: statues and other carvings made of stone or wood and many other artifactsthat people have made. As you would expect, some are talking to each other [as they walk along] and someare silent.

GLAUCON: This is an unusual picture that you are presenting here, and these are unusual prisoners.

SOCRATES: They are very much like us humans, I [Socrates] responded.

What the prisoners see and hear
SOCRATES: What do you think? From the beginning, people like this have never managed, whether on their own or with the help by others, to see anything besides the shadows that are [continually] projected on the wall opposite them by the glow of the fire.

GLAUCON: How could it be otherwise, since they are forced to keep their heads immobile for their entire lives?

SOCRATES: And what do they see of the things that are being carried along [behind them]? Do they not see simply these [namely the shadows]?

GLAUCON: Certainly.

SOCRATES: Now if they were able to say something about what they saw and to talk it over, do you not think that they would regard that which they saw on the wall as beings?

GLAUCON: They would have to.

SOCRATES: And now what if this prison also had an echo reverberating off the wall in front of them [the one that they always and only look at]? Whenever one of the people walking behind those in chains (and carrying the things) would make a sound, do you think the prisoners would imagine that the speaker were anyone other than the shadow passing in front of them?

GLAUCON: Nothing else, by Zeus!

SOCRATES: All in all, I responded, those who were chained would consider nothing besides the shadows of the artifacts as the unhidden.

GLAUCON: That would absolutely have to be.

PART TWO:

THREE STAGES OF LIBERATION

FREEDOM, STAGE ONE

A prisoner gets free
SOCRATES: So now, I replied, watch the process whereby the prisoners are set free from their chains and, along with that, cured of their lack of insight, and likewise consider what kind of lack of insight must be if the following were to happen to those who were chained.

Walks back to the fire
SOCRATES: Whenever any of them was unchained and was forced to stand up suddenly, to turnaround, to walk, and to look up toward the light, in each case the person would be able to do this only with pain and because of the flickering brightness would be unable to look at those things whose shadows he previously saw.

Is questioned about the objects
SOCRATES: If all this were to happen to the prisoner, what do you think he would say if someone were to inform him that what he saw before were [mere] trifles but that now he was much nearer to beings; and that, as a consequence of now being turned toward what is more in being, he also saw more correctly?

The answer he gives
SOCRATES: And if someone were [then] to show him any of the things that were passing by and forced him to answer the question about what it was, don't you think that he would be a wit's end and in addition would consider that what he previously saw [with is own eyes] was more unhidden than what was now being shown [to him by someone else].

GLAUCON: Yes, absolutely.

Looking at the fire-light itself
SOCRATES: And if someone even forced him to look into the glare of the fire, would his eyes not hurt him, and would he not then turn away and flee [back] to that which he is capable of looking at? And would he not decide that [what he could see before without any help] was in fact clearer than what was now being shown to him?

GLAUCON: Precisely.

FREEDOM, STAGE TWO

Out of the cave into daylight
SOCRATES: Now, however, if someone, using force, were to pull him [who had been freed from his chains] away from there and to drag him up the cave's rough and steep ascent and not to let go of him until he had dragged him out into the light of the sun...

Pain, rage, blindness
SOCRATES: ...would not the one who had been dragged like this feel, in the process, pain and rage? And when he got into the sunlight, wouldn't his eyes be filled with the glare, and wouldn't he thus be unable to see any of the things that are now revealed to him as the unhidden?

GLAUCON: He would not be able to do that at all, at least not right away.

Getting used to the light
SOCRATES: It would obviously take some getting accustomed, I think,

if it should be a matter of taking into one's eyes that which is up there outside the cave, in the light of the sun.

Shadows and reflections
SOCRATES: And in this process of acclimatization he would first and most easily be able to look at (1) shadows and after that (2) the images of people and the rest of things as they are reflected in water.

Looking at things directly
SOCRATES: Later, however, he would be able to view (3) the things themselves [the beings, instead of the dim reflections]. But within the range of such things, he might well contemplate what there is in the heavenly dome, and this dome itself, more easily during the night by looking at the light of the stars and the moon, [more easily, that is to say,] than by looking at the sun and its glare during the day.

GLAUCON: Certainly.

FREEDOM, STAGE THREE: THE SUN

Looking at the sun itself
SOCRATES: But I think that finally he would be in the condition to look at (4) the sun itself, not just at its reflection whether in water or wherever else it might appear, but at the sun itself, as it is in and of itself and in the place proper to it and to contemplate of what sort it is.

GLAUCON: It would necessarily happen this way.

Thoughts about the sun: its nature and functions
SOCRATES: And having done all that, by this time he would also be able to gather the following about the sun: (1) that it is that which grants both the seasons and the years; (2) it is that which governs whatever there is in the now visible region of sunlight; and (3) that it is also the cause of all those things that the people dwelling in the cave have before their eyes in some way or other.

GLAUCON: It is obvious that he would get to these things -- the sun and whatever stands in its light-- after he had gone out beyond those previous things, the merely reflections and shadows.

Thoughts about the cave
SOCRATES: And then what? If he again recalled his first dwelling, and the "knowing" that passes as the norm there, and the people with whom he once was chained, don't you think he would consider himself lucky because of the transformation that had happened and, by contrast, feel sorry for them?

GLAUCON: Very much so.

What counts for "wisdom" in the cave
SOCRATES: However, what if among the people in the previous dwelling place, the cave, certain honors and commendations were established for whomever most clearly catches sight of what passes by and also best remembers which of them normally is brought by first, which one later, and which ones at the same time? And what if there were honors for whoever could most easily foresee which one might come by next?

What would the liberated prisoner now prefer?
SOCRATES: Do you think the one who had gotten out of the cave would still envy those within the cave and would want to compete with them who are esteemed and who have power? Or would not he or she much rather wish for the condition that Homer speaks of, namely "to live on the land [above ground] as the paid menial of another destitute peasant"? Wouldn't he or she prefer to put up with absolutely anything else rather than associate with those opinions that hold in the cave and be that kind of human being?

GLAUCON: I think that he would prefer to endure everything rather than be that kind of human being.

PART THREE:

THE PRISONER RETURNS TO THE CAVE

The return: blindness
SOCRATES: And now, I responded, consider this: If this person who had gotten out of the cave were to go back down again and sit in the same place as before, would he not find in that case, coming suddenly out of the sunlight, that his eyes were filled with darkness?"

GLAUCON: Yes, very much so.

The debate with the other prisoners
SOCRATES: Now if once again, along with those who had remained shackled there, the freed person had to engage in the business of asserting and maintaining opinions about the shadows -- while his eyes are still weak and before they have readjusted, an adjustment that would require quite a bit of time -- would he not then be exposed to ridicule down there? And would they not let him know that he had gone up but only in order to come back down into the cave with his eyes ruined -- and thus it certainly does not pay to go up.

And the final outcome:
SOCRATES: And if they can get hold of this person who takes it in hand to free them from their chains and to lead them up, and if they could kill him, will they not actually kill him?

GLAUCON: They certainly will.

The End

Indeed, they did, thus the question before us now and in the future, is what will men do? What will our elite do with all the knowledge gained since the death of Socrates? Will they heed to logic and reason or will they once again try to silence all free thinkers who have raised this alarm bell in an all out effort to lead us to a better world for all.

Printed in the United States
by Baker & Taylor Publisher Services